LEADERSHIP—
MAGIC,
MYTH, OR
METHOD?

Leadership— Magic, Myth, or Method?

J. W. McLean
and
William Weitzel

amacom
American Management Association

The following publishers have generously given permission to use extended quotations from copyrighted works: From *The Female Advantage* by Sally Helgesen. © 1990 by Sally Helgesen. Used by permission of Doubleday, a division of Bantam Doubleday Dell Publishing Group, Inc. From *The Unconscious Conspiracy* by Warren Bennis. Copyright 1976. Reprinted by permission of Warren Bennis. From *Personality Research Form Manual* by D. N. Jackson. Copyright 1984. Used by permission of Sigma Assessment Systems, Port Huron, Mich. From *A History of Economic Thought*. Copyright © 1967 by the Ronald Press Company. Reprinted by permission of John Wiley & Sons, Inc. From *Personality Grid—Managing Interpersonal Relationships* by Larry Wilson. Copyright 1978 by Larry Wilson. All rights reserved. Reprinted by permission of Wilson Learning Corporation. From *Sell-Tell-Jell—Sales Sonics,* by Larry Wilson. Copyright 1969 by Larry Wilson. All rights reserved. Reprinted by permission of Wilson Learning Corporation. From *How to Use Your Physical and Emotional Ability to Overcome Your Problems and Realize Your Goals* by Eugene J. Benge. Copyright 1977 by Dow Jones-Irwin. Reprinted by permission of Business One Irwin. From *Mind of a Manager, Soul of a Leader* by Craig R. Hickman. Copyright © 1990 by John Wiley & Sons, Inc. Reprinted by permission of John Wiley & Sons, Inc. From *Planagement* by Robert M. Randolph. Copyright 1975. Reprinted by permission of Robert M. Randolph. From *Leadership Training* by Lou Heckler. Copyright 1987. Reprinted by permission of Lou Heckler. From *Why Employees Don't Do What They're Supposed to Do* by Ferdinand F. Fournies. Copyright 1988. Reprinted by permission of F. Fournies & Associates, Inc. Excerpt from *Feel the Fear and Do It Anyway* by Susan Jeffers. Copyright © 1987 by Susan Jeffers, reprinted by permission of Harcourt Brace Jovanovich, Inc. From *How's That Again?* by Roger M. D'Aprix. Copyright 1971. Reprinted by permission of Business One Irwin. From *Leaders: The Strategies for Taking Charge* by Warren Bennis & Burt Nanus. Copyright 1985. Reprinted by permission of Warren Bennis.

Library of Congress Cataloging-in-Publication Data

McLean, J. W.
        Leadership—magic, myth or method? / J. W. McLean and William Weitzel.
        p.   cm.
        Includes bibliographical references and index.
        ISBN 0-8144-5054-7
        1. Leadership. 2. Management. I. Weitzel, William. II. Title.
[HD57.7.M396   1992]   91-34595
303.3'4—dc20   CIP

Printing number

10 9 8 7 6 5 4 3 2

Dedicated
to our
exceptional matrimonial leaders
of eighty combined years,
Eleanor and Elizabeth,
who have certainly done
lots of magic.

Contents

Preface

The underlying premise of this book is that the relative scarcity of leadership nearly everywhere is cause for concern and remedial action on the part of political, business, and other organized groups around the world. The need for effective leaders in every walk of life has indeed become critical. But if this situation is to be genuinely improved, we have concluded that the awakening must begin with individuals.

The reassuring message of this book is that leadership does not require unusual talent or that elusive quality we call charisma. Instead, the role of leaders can be stated quite simply: First, they must understand basic leadership principles; and second, they must apply proven leadership skills to the task at hand. To the individual armed with this knowledge and ability, leadership no longer need involve a reckless leap of faith.

The central purpose of this book, therefore, is to challenge you the reader to participate personally by becoming a leader on whatever level is most comfortable to you. For once experienced, even modest success can generate within you a subtle and seductive momentum that will inspire you to lead again and again.

In contemplating the magnitude of this challenge, it has long been fashionable among so-called futurists to warn of the chaotic and accelerating pace of change. They refer to a world gone digital, personal computers that see and hear, seething change in global politics, and more scientific discoveries expected in the next ten years than the world has known in the last thirty thousand years,[1] all happening apace while we struggle to adjust to life in a greenhouse. We prefer

[1]Admiral William J. Crowe, Jr. (retired), addressing the CENTENNIAL LEADERSHIP SYMPOSIA of the University of Oklahoma, Oklahoma City, OK, 2-28-90.

to recall the philosophy of the ancients like Plato, who alluded to the "rediscovery of forgotten truths of the past."[2] We believe one such truth to be the phenomenon of leadership. Indeed, we need not fear the future; the timeless truths of leadership shall prevail.

Meanwhile, a glance at the Table of Contents reveals its key elements:

- Twelve leadership myths; the convenient excuses for playing it safe as a follower
- Six approaches to leadership; a glimpse of some pacesetting studies
- Six fundamental leadership principles; basic tenets upon which leadership is based and leaders may rely
- Six related leadership skills; some of the things leaders need to be able to do
- Six approaches to the application of leadership skills; spanning the chasm between merely understanding and actually applying leadership skills for long-term success
- Evaluating leadership priorities; how the enlightened leader does it

In essence, we present neither an all-inclusive cookbook nor an omniscient bible on leadership; rather, we offer some nonthreatening and enabling approaches to this often elusive and sometimes needlessly complicated subject. The leader/follower phenomenon can obviously involve as few as two individuals or as many as millions. The myths, principles, skills, and application techniques on the following pages can be useful to all who are willing to consider seriously the challenge of leadership and our premise that the awakening must begin with individuals, who really don't need to do magic at all.

---

[2]From an address by the Prince of Wales before the American Institute of Architecture, Washington, D.C., 2-22-90.

Acknowledgments

Writing this book has confirmed how dependent we all are upon so many others every day of our lives.

First, as coauthors, we have depended heavily upon each other, and each of us wishes to lead off with a strong plaudit to the other for his selfless dedication to the project.

Next, we would have been unable to conclude this task without the tireless support of Paula Hill, who carried the major responsibility for typing the manuscript. Also, toward the end of the writing task, Andrea Pope spent some very long days providing us with a conversion of some of our earlier conventionally typed efforts.

Others helped by reading earlier versions and offering insightful suggestions that improved the manuscript immeasurably. Four who were particularly helpful were Ellen Jonsson, Eleanor McLean, Elizabeth Weitzel, and Kathryn Jenson White. A large number of friends contributed ideas, suggestions, and sources of information that shortened our search for supporting documents. These included John Hauch, Dr. Robert Lusch, Charles Rosenblum, Dr. Daniel Wren, and Dr. Herbert Hengst, who steered us into sources related to our discussion of the philosophy of choice.

Intellectual Debts of Coauthor Weitzel

A number of people taught me about the practical side of leadership. From the business arena, two of my former bosses, William A. Hodder and Donald R. Brattain, modeled leadership for me. In the academic arena, my mentors were Onas C. Scandrette, Hjalmar Rosen, and Thomas A. Mahoney, and I was challenged by my fellow students Lynn Anderson, Alan Bass, William K. Graham, and Steven Schwartz, with whom I worked in Fred Fiedler's Group Effectiveness

Lab. My skills in presenting ideas that truly worked came from feedback by my faculty colleagues, especially Ronald J. Burke and Rene V. Dawis, and from countless university students, my subordinates, my consulting clients, as well as thousands of executives, managers, and supervisors with whom I have worked in seminars and training programs over the years. Thanks to all for sending such profound messages.

Intellectual Debts of Coauthor McLean

My tutoring for this book on leadership began, thankfully, more than fifty years ago, when I found myself pressed into what then seemed like a rapid succession of elected and/or appointed offices for which I was ill-prepared: first, on campus; next, on the battlefield; and then, for more than forty years, in banking and in the volunteer world. In reflecting upon each role, what looms very large in my memory is that I invariably had access to one or more sterling leadership models. Names (other than family) that come readily to mind include: Reverend Walter G. Letham, Tony Goetz, B. L. Wertz, Arthur Adams, William Butterfield, V. A. Barbieri, Bryan Grubbs, R. Otis McClintock, R. Elmo Thompson, E. F. Allen, Dillon Anderson, Louis Lundborg, and Rudy Peterson, among the many accomplished leaders whom, fortunately, I have also been able to observe from fairly close range over the years.

In writing this book, we have endeavored to serve jointly as responsible conduits of both relevant information and provocative thought, much of which we, in turn, have in large measure assimilated from others—though we are not attempting to shift the blame for anything that lies in store for our valued readers. Moreover, we have actually resisted the book writing virus for a time, being mindful of Voltaire's quip: " 'Tis far better to remain silent than to increase the number of bad books."

At least, by now, we trust that some will feel we remained silent long enough.

Respectfully,

J. W. McLean
William Weitzel

PART ONE

Understanding the Leadership Mystique: The Myths

(The *Convenient Excuses* for Playing It Safe as a Follower)

> Sometimes, more than knowing what to know is knowing what is just not so.
>
> —Anonymous

There are a number of people in our culture who reject leadership but are unable to say why; still others may know but are unwilling to admit it; and still others only occasionally seem to perceive why. What all these people have in common is that many of their feelings have no basis in reality. This thing called leadership seems to have developed a mystique, so that it is surrounded by complex and almost mystical feelings.

The purpose of this part is to examine the most common myths about leadership and to show that most of the reasons people have for not wanting to be leaders—or for doubting that they have ability to lead—are nonsense. We firmly believe that rejection of the leadership mantle for wrong reasons not only limits an individual's potential but also takes a heavy societal toll. This may account in part for why there has never been a recorded surplus of leaders. However, we can strive for individual awakenings, which in turn might at least check the widening gap between the ravenous need for leadership and the relative scarcity of it. If you're doubtful about your own potential for leadership, read on, keep an open mind, and adapt to the truth.

Leadership Polarity

One of the traditional truths concerning leadership might be called leadership polarity. Have you noted how often a leader is either almost revered or vastly unpopular in the eyes of others? Only a few can remain for very long in limbo between these two opposite poles.

A quick look at the records of U.S. presidents since 1960 makes the case very well. Only one of the last six, Gerald Ford, occupied the 40-to-60 percent mid-range of Gallup Poll popularity for more than twelve months. Each of the others—Reagan, Carter, Nixon, Johnson, and Kennedy—was either below 40 percent or above 60 percent for most of his tenure. No mythology at work here. The aspirant leader should heed this clear dichotomy between those who lead with the genuine acceptance of their followers and those who find themselves at the opposite end of the popularity axis. Followers just don't seem to tolerate mediocrity for very long; hence our term "leadership polarity."

The Dirty Dozen Leadership Myths

In August 1990 we made a survey of U.S. chief executive officers, and, of the twelve mentioned here, Myths 1, 4, and 5 were identified most often as having "given them pause" in their quest for leadership. Next in order were Myths 3 and 6. It is not our purpose by citing these findings to focus in our next few pages only upon these five seemingly most popular excuses for playing it safe as a follower, since another universe of several hundred different respondents might have yielded entirely different results.

Before we consider each of the dozen singly, however, it is interesting to note that one prominent corporate chairman checked eleven of the twelve—all but Myth Two: Leaders Can Never Be Wrong. "If that were so," he wrote in his comments "I wouldn't have lasted twenty-four hours!"

One definition of the term *myth* is ". . . an unscientific belief." Here are twelve for your consideration. We are convinced they are not only unscientific but actually have no validity at all—hence, "the dirty dozen."

Charisma Is a Necessary Leadership Quality

The *Webster's New World Dictionary* definition of *charisma* is "a special quality of leadership that captures the popular imagination and inspires unswerving allegiance and devotion." Another is "a divinely inspired gift . . . or talent." Certainly, such a strong characteristic can have a very positive impact upon a leader's initial effectiveness. Indeed, without such an inborn gift, one might well wonder how effective a leader can be. Those without charisma, many believe, are forever doomed to be mere followers. Fortunately, this is just not so.

Reliance solely upon charisma can, in fact, be the cause of an otherwise effective leader's failure. Even the hint of such a trait is often all that is required for others to rebel. What followers yearn for instead is to be shown how to grow more productive. Leaders who understand this powerful introspective concept best and make certain that it permeates their organizations from the top down are the ones who will enjoy the bountiful rewards of high morale and competitive performance of a self-motivating staff. They will also need little concern for the level of their charismatic qualities.

In his book *The Unconscious Conspiracy*, Dr. Warren Bennis puts it this way:

> There are charismatic people who do not become leaders, and there are non-charismatic people who do. Herbert Hoover, Clement Atlee and Golda Meir come to mind as leaders who have lacked charisma.
>
> There are low-energy leaders and high-energy leaders. There are attractive and unattractive leaders. But all

the accumulated research in personal psychology suggests there is not one single trait or characteristic that would have any value in predicting leadership potentialities. None—not even intelligence.

The perception that leadership requires above-normal *charisma* is simply no longer a realistic excuse for seeking refuge in the ranks of the followers. What a relief it is to know this and to be reassured that no one has been eliminated at birth for whatever leadership role might become appealing along life's way.

MYTH 2

Leaders Can Never Be Wrong

A mistaken but widely used reason for resisting leadership is, "I can't lead, I make mistakes." What a lame excuse!

The popular motivational speaker Charles "Tremendous" Jones has a favorite saying: "You weren't put on earth to make right decisions—you were put here to make decisions and then work like hell to make them right!" Obviously, a leader's long-term success will be enhanced by a decision-making record that is relatively free of mistakes. So, while deliberate mistakes are not recommended, we do suggest instead the realization that:

- Baseball legend Hank Aaron struck out 1,383 times in the process of hitting a record 755 home runs.
- Thomas A. Edison freely spoke of his more than 3,000 laboratory experiments that failed before he finally invented the incandescent lamp.
- John Kreese, prolific author of more than 500 novels, tells his friends that none of his works would ever have come off the press without the nearly 700 rejection slips from which he learned so much.
- Tennessee Williams has said that without having suffered a huge failure on his first play, he would never have written *The Glass Menagerie*.
- Abraham Lincoln was defeated eleven times for public office.

In a very meaningful way, it's important to know that these giants in their respective fields had such imperfect records overall.

What better evidence is there that "leaders can never be wrong" is indeed tiresome mythology? There's nothing dreadful about "being wrong"—everyone is at times. However, if you don't realize when you've made an error or if you stubbornly refused to accept it, you have fallen into an all-too familiar snare.

MYTH 3

Leadership Means Being Consistent

An alibi to which some resort for avoiding leadership roles is the notion that a disciplined consistency is required of the effective leader. How unrealistic!

This does not rule out the fact that consistency is indeed a virtue. In nearly every walk of life, it is a worthy attribute that usually requires great discipline and concentration to attain. But the prevailing myth that consistency above all else is all that matters must be cast aside.

Seasoned leaders know that followers are less concerned with consistency than with being able to know what to expect from those in command. Superior managers all have war stories of how standard operating procedures were forsaken in behalf of a greater goal . . . how their own creative ingenuity won the day . . . or, how ever inconsistent their methodology may have seemed to others at the time, it worked . . . damn it, it worked!

One of the least consistent American generals during World War II was George S. Patton. Yet, he was not really difficult to predict. He aggressively followed whatever strategy was most likely to win the battle. His reputation for tactical resourcefulness and his mastery of formidable logistical challenges were legends. He made it all happen!

In the early spring of 1945, shortly after the rescue of Bastogne, Belgium, following the traumatic Battle of the Bulge, there was an intelligence briefing at Patton's command post, attended by all Third Army unit commanders and their intelligence officers. One of the coauthors was there.

Approximately one second after all were settled in front of him, his eyes flashed upward and he said, "All right men, all I want to do this morning is to go around the room starting right here with you, Colonel Foster, and listen to each commander describe the condition of his unit and what its needs will be as we move out to cross the Rhine in at least three places by April 20. You have 90 seconds each."

Foster made clear that his division was only 70 percent of normal strength because of casualties and frostbite, his ammunition supplies were only fair, and his fuel was marginal. And so it went around the room, with anything but a robust, battle-ready condition reported during the hour and thirty minutes that followed.

No one spoke when the bad news was over. Then the front legs of Patton's chair crashed to the floor and out of it he sprang. "All right, Foster," he bellowed, "you started it—now I'll give you just one minute each to go back around the room and tell me how you mean to solve your so-called problems." What followed was incredible. One by one, a debilitated room full of weary unit commanders was literally transformed into a resourceful team of warriors.

Yes, General Patton's leadership behavior was easily predictable, albeit inconsistent with the norms of the operations manual. Being the leader he was, he sensed the relatively low magnitude of risk, once the Germans were caught in retreat—and he knew that the number of lives saved by ending the war that much sooner was incalculable.

Patton's autocratic style on the battlefield would not be suitable for most peacetime pursuits, but he could be relied upon to respond forcefully to almost any situation. He knew it, his men knew it, and— in time—his enemies came to know it, too. He was indeed predictable, if not always consistent.

MYTH 4

Leaders Should Always Know the Goal in Advance

Except for the most vain among us, who could conceivably feel qualified to fill such an exacting role? Yet, how misguided anyone would be to claim such omnipotence. Would such a zealot succeed as a leader . . . in terms of attracting, holding, and motivating followers?

It's true that some former "captains of industry" did think that way and actually made it work for a time. Harold Geneen, who built ITT into one of the world's biggest corporations, once wrote: "The first obligation of a chief executive is to set the goals for his company . . . point his people in the direction of the goal post and tell them how to get there." But after Geneen's retirement, his great company floundered in a pronounced earnings downtrend. His managers seemingly had little skill at setting their own course.

Even the most conservative old-school management academicians now concede that goal setting must be a collaborative process, if the group is to be held to any degree responsible for the outcome. In his book *Participative Management*, Mark Frohman wrote, "Participative management does not eliminate the executive's role or reduce his accountability for results. Rather, it requires much greater attention to soliciting ideas, encouraging discussion and debate, integrating diverse input, and managing group processes."

The leader, of course, should have sufficient vision to be sensitive to alternative goals that deserve consideration. At times, the leader may even have a strong sense of direction. But true leaders maintain objectivity as they lead their group toward worthwhile, jointly adopted goals and attainable intermediate objectives. One of the by-products of such an open approach may well be the coincidental discovery of one or more candidates for succession to the leader's mantle—candidates who otherwise might never have emerged.

The day has passed—if, indeed, it ever existed—when group goals could be predetermined and force-fed to followers by an all-seeing, all-knowing, autocratic leader. Much has been written of late concerning vision as the sine qua non of leadership. We would distinguish here between unyielding vision and a perceptive sensing of directional alternatives.

MYTH 5

It Is Usually More Stressful to Lead Than to Follow

"Let's always take the least stressful route, by all means," this myth proclaims. But successful leaders disagree. Ask just about any of them how it felt to be a follower, and the typical response is something like: "Even though I'm sometimes much too challenged as a leader, it's far more tolerable than the oppressive stress and uncertainty I knew as a follower."

Never knowing the risks, the rewards for conquering them, or any of the alternative choices can be much more frustrating to the would-be leader than the struggles involved in leadership itself. Can you imagine how stressful it would have been for George Halas to have ended up as assistant manager of the Chicago Bears, for Douglas MacArthur to have been stuck as an administrative colonel in the U.S. Army, or for Golda Meir to have remained a backbencher in the Israel parliament? The belief that it's less stressful to follow than to lead has no rightful place in the psyche of the fledgling leader. Veteran comic Milton Berle would say it differently: "Only the lead dog of a team of Alaskan huskies enjoys a change of scenery!"

The Leader Must Be Able to Perform the Jobs of the Followers

This may be true in an embryonic family business, but in this increasingly complex world, there just wouldn't be any leaders at all if this shallow myth were valid.

Today, it is virtually unthinkable that any straw boss, foreman, or executive could deliver acceptable standards of performance of all the duties under his or her command. There's an old Scottish saying that makes the point eloquently: "Whatsoever is rightfully done— however humble—is noble." The enlightened leader knows that many of such duties can best be performed by others.

This is not to say that proficiency in a wide variety of skills is a handicap to the leader. Indeed, in the U.S. armed forces those who aspire to be commissioned officers must first learn the skills of buck privates at training camp. By so doing, they gain indispensable insight for use as commanders later. However, those who opt to follow rather than to lead because they haven't mastered all the jobs to be performed by the group make a tragic error in judgment.

One of the coauthors was troubled by this myth early in his career when he made the shift from investment banking to commercial banking. Almost immediately, he became a loan officer. The job was an exhilarating step forward, but he was troubled that others with his rank had had much more experience, having come up the hard way. Would his noticeably favored treatment deny him the acceptance of his peers? As it turned out, not at all. The group was open and generous, an outcome that can be attributed at least in part to his free admission going in that he had "never done servitude in the lower ranks of the bank and he would probably not last very long in his new job, without a lot of help from those who had."

MYTH 7

A Leader in One Environment Should Lead in Others

This myth is not without some foundation. More opportunities are open to those who have led successfully in one realm to step forward in others. The ability to do more than one thing well is often the difference between competence and excellence. Take the case of Winston Churchill (where perhaps the difference was between excellence and brilliance). As a war correspondent, he won renown for his courage. As an outspoken cabinet minister who held many portfolios including that of first lord of the admiralty, he championed many important causes. As an historian, his Nobel Prize was the first ever awarded for the quality of both the spoken as well as the written word. As prime minister, he personified the will of his people leading Britain to her finest hour.

But the opportunities for multiple leadership roles are only that—opportunities—and no one is obliged to pursue them.

In a penetrating article by Thomas E. Cronin in the *Presidential Studies Quarterly*, there are some helpful observations:

> Can an effective leader in one situation transfer this capacity, this skill, this style—to another setting? The record is mixed indeed. Certain persons have been effective in diverse settings. George Washington and Dwight Eisenhower come to mind. Jack Kemp and Bill Bradley, two well known and respected members of Congress, were previously successful professional athletes. Scores of business

leaders have been effective in the public sector and vice versa. Scores of military leaders have become effective in business or politics; some in both. However, there are countless examples of those who have not met with success when they have tried to transfer their leadership abilities from one setting to a distinctly different setting.

What often happens, of course, is that some leaders simply can't resist carrying their mantle from one relationship to another, from business to club to church. Such compulsive people are sometimes thought to be more than a little overbearing.

On the other hand, there are many who refuse to get on board the leadership trolley for fear they will be involuntarily taken for ride after ride. Therein lies the mythology. For leadership need not be an insatiable, inner-driven compulsion. Those who make it appear that way, however effective they may have been in their multiple realms, are being counterproductive to societal needs. Enlisting new leaders is tough enough even without the mythical fear that a single "take-charge" commitment will only bring on one new imposition after another.

MYTH 8

Leadership Is an Opportunity Only for Those Who Have Strong Support From the "Higher-Ups"

How discouraging and even debilitating it can be to wonder whether competence and productivity will lose out in the end to cronyism. Under such circumstances, there is indeed a compelling inclination to rechannel one's energies in other directions, unfettered by favoritism. Obviously, to hang in there year after year after year, experiencing one career disappointment after another, is futile.

But there's another strategy, a superior one. It begins with the conviction that in most enlightened organizations "pull from higher-ups" will rarely defeat fierce dedication and plain old capability. In fact, some of those who have enjoyed influence on high have seen such favoritism contribute to failure in the final outcome.

The issue of nepotism is right on point here. How often have the filial ambitions of a company president and proud father outrun the capacity and capability of his inept offspring! In most of these embarrassing cases, it doesn't take long for the unqualified family member to leave the company.

Of course, there are times when such a transfer of power works and the young people apply their own leadership skills admirably to

18

the job. One notable example is the fascinating saga of International Business Machines. IBM grew into one of the world's premier corporations under the powerful leadership of Thomas Watson, Sr., and the company's status was augmented by the efforts of his talented son, Thomas Watson, Jr.

MYTH 9

Followers Resent Being Manipulated

The underlying assumption here is that effective leadership is nothing more or less than manipulation of followers to do the leader's bidding. On the contrary, truly effective leadership is all about motivation, not manipulation. Of course, dictators like Hitler and Stalin not only manipulated people but have also been responsible for the deaths of millions. The famous words of Lord Acton bear repeating here: "All power tends to corrupt, and absolute power corrupts absolutely."

Motivation (which will be dealt with in some depth in Parts Three and Four) must be clearly distinguished from manipulation. An old friend and raconteur, Fred Setser of Tulsa, tells a story that makes the point in an unforgettable way!

"The family station wagon is speeding on a poor trail through the back woods when—suddenly—it enters an unexpected clearing bounded on one side by the trail and on the other by a picturesque stream. The father slams on the brakes; all four doors open simultaneously; he and the oldest son begin erecting the tent; and the other two boys scurry off after kindling, while mother and daughter begin laying out the fixin's for the evening meal. All is prepared in record time. Then, from a couple of hundred yards downstream, comes a shout: "How do you do it?"

"Do what?" asks Dad.

"How on earth does your family arrive forty minutes after mine and you're already set for chow?"

"Very simple."

"How do you mean?" he shouts.

"I mean motivation," yells Dad.

"How's that?" he begs.

"Well, it's very simple," says Dad again. "You see, I just tell my bunch that nobody goes to the bathroom until all the chores are done."

Now, was this family motivated or manipulated? Our answer is that this was motivation in its purest form. What the father knew best was that his family would be enormously proud of the finished product: a model campsite, pulled together in record time, clean and trim for everyone, primarily themselves, to see and admire. The "bathroom threat" was merely a catalyst to get them all started.

Do not shrink from leadership for fear of becoming manipulative. Genuine motivation, once experienced, is far too rewarding; besides, you will soon learn that anything that smacks of manipulation won't even get off the ground.

Leadership Is Often Incidental Because the Success or Failure of Most Group Efforts Is Determined by Outside Events

Throughout recorded history, there have been outside events of enormous magnitude that have had a formidable impact upon people's lives. But to assume from this that success or failure at leadership is entirely out of a leader's hands would be tragic. Being adrift like a note corked in a bottle cast in the ocean would be a better fate. At least bottled notes can be found and the writer conceivably identified and contacted. Put another way, if you surrender to mediocrity and take refuge in indifference, you will be just one face among many in the shiftless crowds on the sidelines.

Even worse, some of what we read and hear in the daily news holds little promise of a trend reversal. When former Secretary of Education Lauro Cavazos unveiled the National Assessment of Educational Progress (NAEP) Report, a twenty-year analysis of student performance at all levels in the United States, the nation was put on notice that it was intellectually at risk. The composite report card gave poor grades to American public school students in reading, writing, mathematics, science, U.S. history, civics, and geography; it also found that, for the two decades under study, all improvement lines were nearly flat. It's as if the entire country was marking time, just waiting for some outside event to come along and be the catalyst for change in education. Of course, it's clear that when and if the U.S. educational system is improved, it will not be because of some fortuitous outside agency or event. Rather, it will be because an outraged and motivated citizenry has been awakened from complacency by those among them who refused to buy the myth that their efforts to show the way would be useless until the occurrence of some unforeseen favorable event.

MYTH 11

Leaders Are an Endangered Species

In a free-market economy, leaders have every chance not only to succeed but also to fail. It is no secret that the average tenure of the chief executives of Fortune 500 companies is well under five years. It is also true that most of these careers close with laudable retirement, not abysmal failure.

For obvious reasons, however, the publicity that accompanies the decline of a business or political leader seems to make an indelible imprint on the public. Most (if not all) leaders have their detractors, who always enjoy seeing them toppled. Somehow, because there seem to be regular reports in the media of such negative events, one is quite logically persuaded—if only subconsciously—that to lead is to be endangered. This unfortunate mind-set is hardly a plus for leadership—it also happens to be grossly flawed.

Are we too prone to accept what we read without ever questioning the twist or spin of the journalist? The now retired intellectual senator from California, S. I. Hayakawa, put it this way: "If you see in any given situation only what everybody else can see, you can be said to be so much a representative of your culture that you may be a victim of it."

For your consideration, then, we submit that if you really believe leadership is an endangered way of life, you may well be a "victim" of "your culture." In our view, the "endangered" are the complacent followers who are content to let leadership go by default.

Leadership Is Just Too Complicated for Me

Insecurity is far from uncommon, even among accomplished leaders, but this kind of self-deprecation borders on masochism. In the Preface, we suggested that leadership is an "often elusive and sometimes needlessly complicated subject." We have found this myth to be a formidable hurdle not only among many proven leaders but also among some of the best students on campus. Is leadership really "too complicated," or is this just a convenient veil to mask our inner fears of leading?

There seems to be a paradox here. Quite often, those who suffer most from this self-inflicted curse have the least to fear. Psychologists say that many successful people feel anxiety because they are fierce perfectionists. Thomas Harrison of the Phobia Center of the Southwest in Dallas tells his clients who fight paralysis at the podium, "You wouldn't have this problem if you'd just go ahead and screw up more."

Is it all, then, merely a matter of attitude? Instead of a tiresome sermonette on attitude, we suggest that—whatever complications you encounter, real or imagined—the process of leading really is merely a matter of applying some proven skills that are rooted in some very basic leadership principles.

Throughout the remainder of this book, and especially in Part Six (where we will be discussing how an enlightened leader evaluates his or her leadership priorities), this thesis concerning attitude will recur.

In summary, these twelve myths are only poor excuses for spurning the mantle of leadership. On the other hand, there are some legitimate leadership risks that can be quite costly and, accordingly, should be carefully evaluated by those who aspire to lead. Here are a half-dozen that deserve both inspection and reflection:

- Fear of failure
- Fear of embarrassment
- Fear of disappointing others
- Fear of resentment by current leaders
- Lack of respect for current leaders
- Lack of self-confidence

Only a few paragraphs earlier, we referred to anxiety disorders. Can these words be too harsh to apply to honest fears and genuine feelings of inferiority? Should these six stumbling blocks be casually dismissed? The coauthors don't dismiss them at all, especially since we've known them all too well ourselves. We do, however, believe that at the very core of these fears and all their cousins is basic insecurity, which we have already addressed in Myth Twelve. Moreover, every subsequent page of this book shall be dedicated to enhancing the reader's resolve to give leadership a safe and secure try. In the words of Eleanor Roosevelt, "No one can make you feel inferior— without your consent."

Lucky Thirteen

Before we bring Part One to a close, we submit for consideration what might have been Myth Thirteen. It didn't make the original list simply because we cannot document our conviction that it is entirely without foundation. This dichotomy will become clearer; but first, what might have been Myth Thirteen: "They'll Never Accept a Woman Leader."

Those who forfeit their chances for leadership with this rationale are of course not alone. Indeed, entirely too much of the world at large has given it credibility over the years. But there is now a formidable and growing array of evidence to the contrary. The ascendancy of women in every profession, as heads of state, and even among some former bastions of male chauvinism has been one of the prime megatrends of the current century.

In her recent book, *Female Advantage*, Sally Helgesen contrasts working patterns of the men and women she surveyed, as follows:

Men	*Women*
1. Worked at an unrelenting pace, with no breaks in activity during the day	1. Worked at a steady pace, but with small breaks scheduled throughout the day
2. Their days were characterized by interruption, discontinuity, and fragmentation	2. Did not view unscheduled tasks and encounters as interruptions
3. Spared little time for activities not directly related to work	3. Made time for activities not directly related to their work
4. Exhibited a preference for live action encounters	4. Preferred live action encounters, but scheduled time to attend to mail
5. Maintained a complex network of relationships with people outside their organizations	5. Maintained a complex network of relationships with people outside their organizations
6. Immersed in the day-to-day need to keep the company going, they lacked time for reflection	6. Focused on the ecology of leadership
7. Identified themselves with their jobs	7. Saw their own identities as complex and multifaceted
8. Had difficulty sharing information	8. Scheduled time for sharing information

Helgesen based her conclusions about male executives on the pioneering study made by Henry Mintzberg in 1968.

In commenting on Mintzberg's work, which included minute-by-minute diary studies of five male executives, another management scholar, Jeffrey Sommenfeld, Director of the Center for Leadership and Career Change at Emory University in Atlanta, wrote

> Mintzberg changed the way people looked at management. Before him, the formal aspects had been considered most important—the planning, the organizing, the long-range stuff. The whole picture was very static, emphasizing what a manager got accomplished; for example, if he got a labor contract signed. But Mintzberg put the emphasis on what the manager *did* to get that contract, the actual tasks and behaviors, the management by walking around.

Sally Helgesen found a number of subtle differences between the working patterns of men and women. Is it possible that the dichotomy between woman's "ecology of leadership" and man's lack of "time for reflection" accounts for one of the most remarkable mega-trends of the last two decades, the advancement of women on all fronts? Of course, the answer to this question is far less important than the wider recognition, finally, of what has happened to women as heads of state, in politics generally, in business, in the professions, and in the arts. Yes, women are definitely getting there!

Statistics published by the U.S. Department of Commerce in 1990 indicate how things changed during the 1980s.

- The number of women-owned businesses in the United States ballooned 57 percent from 1982 to 1987, from 2.6 million to 4.1 million.
- This rate of growth was more than four times greater than the 14 percent overall growth rate for all businesses during the same period.
- More than 40 percent of the new businesses formed in the United States during the first half of 1990 were started by women.
- In 1989, about 30 percent of all U.S. businesses—more than four million—were owned by women. These businesses earned a total of $280 billion during that year.

One-third of all MBA degrees awarded by U.S. institutions last year were earned by women. The circulation of the magazine *Working Woman* is second only to the *Wall Street Journal* among business-oriented publications. More and more women are running for political office, too:

- Ten of thirty-four U.S. governorships in 1990 were contested by women.
- The United States already has three women governors. Some say that figure will rise to eighteen or nineteen by the year 2000.
- In the nation's fourth largest city, Houston, the mayor, the police chief, the superintendent of schools, and the presidents of the Chamber of Commerce and the University of Houston are all women.

Such figures and facts should no longer shock anyone. The fact is that women can be effective leaders in spite of the lingering obstacles against them. And this brings us full circle to our myth, "They'll never follow a woman." You see, it simply can't be a myth until it no longer has the slightest credibility. And, again, we believe there is a growing body of evidence that women really are getting there.

But the Perception Persists

Our Part One has been about exploding some tired old myths concerning leadership. Naturally, a few are more ingrained than others in the public psyche. Indeed, who can say at any given time which are the more predominant?

What we do know instead is that the popular perception persists that those who dare to lead are engaged in a perilous effort. A popular cartoon makes the point in an unforgettable way. The leading gander of a flight of geese in V-formation is shown colliding with a flagpole. The caption reads: "The Hazards of Leadership."

While some who opt to lead have, indeed, experienced head-on collisions at times, it is our view that this is a highly erroneous perception of leadership generally. This belief must be met and neutralized if the growing leadership deficit is to be checked. The remainder of this book is committed to that purpose.

PART TWO

A Glimpse of Some Cardinal Leadership Studies

(Pacesetting Efforts That Have Gone Before)

Hindsight is the only true vision.

—Anonymous

The study of leadership has fascinated philosophers, writers, and scholars down through the ages. Most histories have been based, at least in part, on the lives and actions of kings and queens, presidents and generals, and all the others who have led their nations and peoples since time immemorial. In our modern era, as historians have turned away from the "great man" method of inquiry, psychologists and other social scientists have intensified their studies of leaders in all walks of life.

From among all of the work in the area of leadership we have put together a brief, highly selective, carefully considered overview of the subject, from the political philosophy of Socrates and Plato to the contemporary models that form the bases of so many college and university courses.

This survey is not complete or comprehensive—that would require another book much larger in size than this volume. But here in Part Two we wanted to present the important building blocks that formed the foundation of the Principles, Skills, and Applications that we offer in subsequent parts.

Socratic Philosophy

(The "Philosopher King" Concept)

Studies on sociocultural leadership seem to focus upon what has become known as the Socratic method for their point of departure. Socrates wrote nothing himself. We can thank his students, however, and a legion of followers, especially Plato, for enunciating his ageless beliefs.

Ironically, to many students of ancient philosophy, Plato's manuscripts were something of a mystery. His style is difficult and sometimes obscures his meaning; even greater problems of comprehension stem from the structure of the dialogues presented in the *Republic* and in his last work; the twelve books of the *Laws.*

The purpose of this inquiry is to seek access to Plato's explanation of the "philosopher king" concept, which most scholars attribute to the earlier teachings of Socrates. As the noted scholar William Cranston Lawton observed in 1901: "How much of these wonderful dialogues is Socratic and how much is Platonic can never be fully answered."

Republic Versus *Laws*

It was fashionable for philosophers during Plato's time to espouse their societal beliefs through the presentation of a model city, which would embody their ideal order of living.

In Plato's *Republic*, all governmental power was entrusted to the sovereignty of "guardians," who had undergone long training in philosophy and developed a deep concern for the well-being of the governed. More recently, the term "benevolent monarch" has come to describe such rulers. Plato used the term "philosopher king."

As scholars of the time began to challenge the "philosopher king" concept on grounds of impracticality, Plato reported that Socrates said, "It does not matter whether the state [described in the *Republic*] does or will exist. It is a pattern set up in heaven on which whoever wishes may model himself . . . there could be such a state if philosophers become kings or kings philosophers.

Thus, all people should aspire to idealistic values. This concept formed the basis for later writings by Plato known as the *Statesman*. According to that work, "Since true statesmen know what is best for their cities, it does not matter whether they act with or without law, whether they are rich or poor, or whether their subjects do or do not consent." This trend of thought would suggest that all a people need do is keep a weather eye out for the "true statesman."

In Plato's *Laws*, on the other hand, ultimate governance of the model city was supposed to rest with the law rather than with any particular group of citizens. There was much less emphasis placed on the need for philosophical training because all citizens—not just a select few—were expected to take part in a more democratic governance. Putting Plato's *Republic* together with his *Laws*, we see that the concept of the "philosopher king" remains valid as a theoretical ideal, but the rule of law is advisable in practice.

A final characteristic of the "philosopher king" was espoused by Plato in his letter VII, in which he also recalls the death of Socrates and its discouraging impact upon his earlier notions of becoming active politically: "He concluded that the trouble of the human race would not cease until either those who were true lovers of wisdom achieved political office, or those who held political power became lovers of wisdom themselves. The "philosopher king"—though all-powerful—is not a tyrant at all but the benevolent statesman who is inherently an avowed lover of wisdom.

While all of this evolved nearly four hundred years before Christ, how remarkable it is to find this same "benevolent statesmanship" thesis at the core of our Studies 2 through 6, which follow more than twenty centuries later.

STUDY 2

Murray/Maslow/
Alderfer/McClelland

("Need Hierarchy")

Just as surely as the study of leadership inevitably introduces motivation, one does not probe in this field for long without a headlong encounter with what has been called the need hierarchy theory of motivation. The concept of human need is one of the most pervasive and powerful notions available for study in all of the available writings on leadership.

In business, for example, the generation of greater earning power and greater sales revenue will, in the long run, depend upon the knowledge that customers do not buy merely products and services, but benefits sought in the form of solutions to problems created by their needs.

The implications of this for managers and leaders alike are at once both sobering and intriguing. One inference might be to become a needs scholar, and all else shall be added unto you. However simplistic this approach may be, it is nevertheless worthy of consideration. Here we shall review the contributions of four needs scholars whose collective works have garnered a wide following among leaders in numerous fields of endeavor.

Murray's Manifest Needs Theory

In 1938, based upon several years of clinical observations by the Harvard Psychological Clinic, Henry A. Murray wrote his classic *Explora-*

tions in Personality. His thesis was that individuals could be classified according to various personality-need variables, each believed to represent central motivation. A need was defined as "a force . . . in the brain region . . . which organizes perception, appreciation, intellect, conation and action in such a way as to transform . . . an unsatisfying situation."

Murray held that needs were not something that could be observed by the researcher. Rather, *needs* analysis was "a hypothetical process, the occurrence of which is imagined in order to account for certain objective and subjective facts." In other words, one could only infer needs from observed behavior.

Moreover, needs were viewed by Murray as largely learned behavior—rather than innate tendencies—activated by external cues and composed of two principal factors: first, a qualitative component or object toward which the motive is directed; second, a quantitative component representing the intensity of the need/motive toward the object.

Murray recognized, too, that an individual's personality could be composed of numerous divergent and often conflicting needs, each having the potential for motivating behavior, and that at different times all these needs could be either manifest ("activated") or latent. The latter does not imply that such needs are weak, only that they have been inhibited.

An alphabetical listing of Murray's so-called manifest needs includes the following:

Achievement: Aspires to accomplish difficult tasks; maintains high standards and is willing to work toward distant goals; responds to competition; is willing to put forth effort to attain excellence.

Affiliation: Enjoys being with friends and people in general; accepts people readily; makes efforts to win friendships and maintain associations with people.

Aggression: Enjoys combat and argument; easily annoyed; sometimes willing to hurt people to get his or her own way; may seek to "get even" with people perceived as having harmed him or her.

Autonomy: Tries to break away from restraints, confinement, or restrictions of any kind; enjoys being unattached, free, not tied to people, places, or obligations; may be rebellious when faced with restraints.

Endurance: Willing to work long hours; doesn't give up quickly on a problem; persevering, even in the face of great difficulty; patient and unrelenting in work habits.

Exhibition: Wants to be the center of attention; enjoys having an audience; engages in behavior that wins the notice of others; may enjoy being dramatic or witty.

Harm avoidance: Does not enjoy exciting activities, especially if danger is involved; avoids risk of bodily harm; seeks to maximize personal safety.

Impulsivity: Tends to act on the spur of the moment and without deliberation; gives vent readily to feelings and wishes; speaks freely; may be volatile in emotional expression.

Nurturance: Gives sympathy and comfort; assists others whenever possible; interested in caring for children, the disabled, or the infirm; offers a "helping hand" to those in need; readily performs favors for others.

Order: Concerned with keeping personal effects and surroundings neat and organized; dislikes clutter, confusion, lack of organization; interested in developing methods for keeping materials methodically organized.

Power: Attempts to control the environment and to influence or direct other people; expresses opinions forcefully; enjoys the role of leader and may assume it spontaneously.

Succorance: Frequently seeks the sympathy, protection, love, advice, and reassurance of other people; may feel insecure or helpless without such support; confides difficulties readily to a receptive person.

Understanding: Wants to understand many areas of knowledge; values synthesis of ideas, verifiable generalization, logical thought, particularly when directed at satisfying intellectual curiosity.[1]

Maslow's Need Hierarchy Theory

Unlike Murray, Brandeis University Professor Abraham H. Maslow did not rely on research evidence to support his theory on human needs. The popularity of Maslow's Theory, which he advanced in the 1950s, is related partly to its convenient classification of basic human

[1]Adapted from D. N. Jackson, *Personality Research Form Manual* (Port Huron, Mich.: Sigma Assessments, Inc., 1984).

needs in the form of a triangular hierarchy and partly to the logical and easily understood notion that all human behavior results from motivation based upon human need. In ascending order of prepotency, Maslow's hierarchy of needs consists of five categories of need, as illustrated in Figure 1.

In addressing the hierarchy, Maslow declared two fundamental premises:

1. Once a certain need is satisfied, it loses potency as a motivating force until it is once again activated.
2. Once lower needs are met, the individual moves up the hierarchy one level at a time.

As a theory of motivation, Maslow also utilized the two concepts of deprivation and gratification to link needs to behavior. The best short explanation of Maslow's theory that we have read is in a 1988 research paper, entitled "Motivation and Work Behavior," written by Richard M. Steers and Lyman Porter:

> He postulated that deprivation or dissatisfaction of a need of high prepotency will lead to the domination of this need over the organism's personality.
>
> Following the satisfaction of a dominating need, the second element of the dynamic force in Maslow's Theory will then take place. Relative gratification of a given need submerges it and "activates" the next higher need in the hierarchy. The activated need then dominates and organizes the individual's personality and capacities so that instead of the individual's being hunger obsessed, he now becomes safety obsessed.
>
> This process of deprivation → domination → gratification → activation continues until the physiological, safety, affiliation, and esteem needs have all been gratified and the self-actualization need has been activated. In a

Figure 1. Maslow's hierarchy of needs.

Need for self-actualization
Self-esteem needs
Belongingness needs
Safety needs
Psychological needs

later work, Maslow modified the gratification idea by proposing that gratification of the self-actualization need
causes an increase in its importance rather than a decrease.

In 1962, Maslow was a consultant at the Del Mar, California, plant of
Non-Linear Systems, Inc. It was his first contact with an industrial
application of the managerial psychology of motivation and productivity. When theory meets practice, the results are not always congen-
ial. Nevertheless, Maslow concluded that practical application did indeed support and confirm the validity of his initial theoretical work
and he said so, proudly, in his book *Eupsychian Management*. (The
word *eupsychian* in the book's title was defined by Maslow as "the
culture that would be generated by 1,000 self-actualized people on
some sheltered island where they would not be interfered with.")

Between Maslow's visit and the publication of his book, Non-
Linear Systems experienced a sharp contraction in the demand for its
products. Accordingly, Maslow wrote in his preface that "these principles hold primarily for good conditions rather than stormy
weather."

Included in his good conditions were thirty-six assumptions necessary for the theory to work, exemplified by the following:

- Everyone can be trusted.
- Everyone is to be fully informed.
- Everyone has the same urge to achieve.
- Everyone will recognize the same managerial objectives, re-
  gardless of their level or status in the organization.
- Everyone will work with goodwill rather than rivalry or jeal-
  ousy.
- Everyone shall enjoy good teamwork.

Maslow also wrote of his dissatisfaction with management literature on leadership itself. He confessed that his life would "become
totally meaningless" if he were not a psychologist and that his total
identification with psychology is an aspect of what he calls "the B-
values" and "the B-leadership" in us all to respond to the over-arch-
ing one-big-value confronting us at any given time. He appealed for
recognition by all who would lead that their effectiveness and success
is related directly to their ability to:

exert consistent B-POWER . . . a selfless devotion to the
object requirements of the situation . . . with absolutely no
kick out of being able to order people around . . . to with-

stand hostility . . . perhaps to be unpopular without falling apart . . . to say "no" . . . to inflict pain if necessary . . . not be ruled by fear . . . be impervious to retaliation . . . with no need to be loved . . . even to be laughed at . . . and, above all, a capacity to succeed without maudlin celebration.

Alderfer's Modified Need Hierarchy Theory

In 1969, Clayton Alderfer proposed a "modified need hierarchy theory," which essentially collapsed Maslow's five hierarchical levels into three. This model has since become known as the existence–relatedness–growth theory (ERG), summarized as follows:

- *Existence needs* are those required to sustain human existence, and include both Maslow's physiological and safety needs.
- *Relatedness needs* are those concerning how people interact with others and their surroundings, and include Maslow's belongingness needs.
- *Growth needs* are those that represent people's highest ambitions, and include Maslow's needs for both self-esteem and self-actualization.

Alderfer's theory differed from Maslow's original formulation, in two major respects. First, when one is continually denied need gratification, lower needs tend to reemerge; he called this frustration regression. Second, more than one need may be operative at the same time.

McClelland's Simplified Thesis

In 1971, David C. McClelland defined need as "a recurrent concern for a goal state" and declared that "needs were not something that could be observed (and/or measured) by researchers."

The studies McClelland directed found that there was a strong correlation between high need for achievement (*N* Achievement) and high levels of performance. More recent studies have tended to support such a conclusion. Those driven by *N* Achievement tend to set tough goals; they enjoy taking personal responsibility and risking new ventures. In short, they are more objective than subjective.

McClelland also probed the earlier work of Alderfer that saw power as the major goal of all human endeavor. Although McClelland did not confirm Alderfer's findings, he nevertheless recognized that the need for power (*N* Power) is important. Those to whom this need is key are generally more subjective than objective. The stereotypical manifestation of *N* Power is one who attempts to influence directly through strong opinions, frequent suggestions, constant persuasion, and other domineering tactics.

McClelland noted that *N* Power can take two forms among managers: personal power and institutional power. He argued persuasively that managers with a high need for institutional power are superior to those with personal power needs alone or high *N* Achievement types. However, he also found, surprisingly, that managers with high need for achievement tended to be more participative, allowing subordinates to have a greater voice.

What this suggests to us is that superior leaders can emerge from either group (*N* Achievement or *N* Power), given a reasonably thorough exposure to the leadership principles, skills, and application techniques which we shall advance in this book.

Austrian School of Economics

(Drucker's "MBO")

The so-called Austrian school of economics was not an institution of higher learning even though it did have its students—or perhaps followers would be a better term. The Austrian school includes those who embraced the teachings of a number of European free market economists who flourished in the late nineteenth and early twentieth centuries.

Joseph Alois Schumpeter, who has been called "one of the great economists of all time," was a notable member of this school. He was highly versed in mathematics, statistics, political and social philosophy, and economic history. But his great strength was his mastery of the entire scope of economics.

Born in 1883 in what is now Czechoslovakia, Schumpeter came to Harvard in 1924 and remained there for nearly twenty years. He was president of the American Economic Association in 1949. His best-known book is *The Theory of Economic Development*, and his *History of Economic Analysis* is ranked as one of the greatest works in the field.

We feature him here because of his acknowledged grasp of the entire framework of economic thought and structure since 1800 and his contributions to free market economic literature. Schumpeter's major contributions to the study of leadership are found in his theory of the entrepreneur as the prime mover in economic activity. In his book *A History of Economic Thought*, John Fred Bell summarized Schumpeter's work in this area as follows:

> Goods flow in one direction as a stream to the consumers, while money flows in the opposite direction from the consumer back to the producer, who employs it again in production. . . . Every new element of growth rests upon a preceding one and this in turn sets up conditions for subsequent development. Development is therefore a continuous process of growth; a dynamic movement "which forever alters and displaces the equilibrium state previously existing. Our theory of development is nothing but a treatment of this phenomenon and the processes incident to it." Provision is made for the entrepreneur who carries out the new combinations in production. This may be made on either a small or a large scale; hence a leadership function is assumed which is important. The entrepreneur becomes an innovator.

These references to entrepreneurship and leadership could have been written today, calculated to usher in a twenty-first-century mentality for streamlining the world's economic environment.

Peter F. Drucker and MBO

Schumpeter's stand concerning the essential roles of economic growth, profit, and capital accumulation in a circular flow—with a heightened awareness of the cyclicality of business conditions—afforded a logical launching pad for the work of the Austrian-American economist, Peter F. Drucker. Drucker, like Schumpeter, saw society and business in "a constant state of creation, growth, stagnation, and decline," according to the economist Daniel A. Wren. "What keeps an organization from failing is its ability to perform the entrepreneurial tasks of innovating—finding a new or better product, creating new customers or uses for old or new products, and making pricing, or distributing the product or service in a more competitive way."

While Drucker has been generally credited with the theory of management by objectives (MBO), he himself maintained that MBO was not new, having been practiced earlier at General Electric by Harold Smiddy, at General Motors by Alfred P. Sloan, Jr., and at DuPont by Pierre du Pont and Donaldson Brown.

Perhaps what Drucker did most for the MBO concept is highlighted in his most popular book, *The Practice of Management.* It is here that he examines how business objectives should be set and by whom

. . . the proper use of reports and monitoring procedures . . . and the multiplied strength of participatory goal setting.

We close this portion of Part Two with the words of psychologist Kurt Lewin, "There is nothing so practical as good theory," and the "flipside" by Daniel A. Wren: "Perhaps the future of management education may lie in our discovering that there is nothing so theoretical as good practice."

Part Three will show how the Austrian School of Economics—and Drucker's MBO in particular—provided a solid foundation for our own Master Planning Model (MPM), the key element of our Leadership Principle 5.

The Ohio State Studies

(The Contingency Approach)

The classic Ohio State studies (in the late 1940s and early 1950s) were the precursors of most of today's situational leadership concepts. Situational leadership itself may be characterized as the doctrine that a leader's style should be modified according to the variable circumstances encountered.

There are basically two approaches to situational leadership. Some theorists hold, in effect, that "situational relativity is a matter of individual fine tuning . . . by the leader . . . nothing more . . . and there is little reason to consider situational differences."* Those who downplay the situation are known as *noncontingency* theorists; familiar names in this area include Lipert's System 4, McGregor's Theory Y, Ouchi's Theory Z, and Blake and Mouton's 9–9 Leadership Style. Each of these espouse the view that there is one best approach to managing that is universal in its application.

Other leadership theorists have put forth specific ways in which styles of leadership should be related directly to situational requirements. Those who lean in this direction are said to follow the *contingency* approach.

Fiedler's Contingency Model

In 1967, Dr. F. E. Fiedler introduced a deceptively simple personality test for leaders, asking them to think of the person with whom they

---

*This quotation and much of the information in this section come from a book by Victor H. Vroom and Arthur H. Jago, *The New Leadership* (Englewood Cliffs, N.J.: Prentice Hall, 1988).

"could work least well." Fiedler then asked the leader to rate that individual on a set of eight-point scales anchored at either end by a set of opposites, such as pleasant–unpleasant, friendly–unfriendly. This measure is called the Least Preferred Co-Worker Scale (LPC). Leaders who describe their LPCs in relatively unfavorable terms are said to be task motivated; similarly, leaders who describe their LPCs in relatively favorable terms are said to be relationship motivated.

At first, Fiedler described task-motivated leaders as autocratic and relationship-motivated leaders as participative. He later acknowledged this to be an oversimplification, as attempts to apply the theory across a wide spectrum—to basketball teams, to army tank crews, to open-hearth furnace workers, etc.—yielded spotty results. In some instances, high-LPC leaders were highest in performance; in others, they were low performers. According to Vroom and Jago,

> Fiedler found that much of this apparent inconsistency could be explained by classifying the three dimensions: (1) the degree of structure involved in the group task; (2) the amount of power given to the leader by virtue of his or her position, and (3) the quality of interpersonal relationships between the leader and other members. To Fielder, these dimensions have one thing in common. Each pertains to a different aspect of the "favorableness of the situation." Thus, a highly favorable situation is characterized by high-task structure, high-position power, and positive leader–member relationship.

Other leadership scholars have written that when these factors are either all favorable or all unfavorable, task-oriented leaders should perform best. When they are mixed or intermediate, relationship-oriented leaders should perform best.

As the first and most prominent contingency model, the LPC has continued to generate both interest and controversy. Skeptics fault Fiedler's approach on the ground that it provides little guidance to leaders seeking to carry out their roles more effectively. We agree with this criticism, since the focus of this book is on leader behavior and its disciplined modification when necessary, rather than on leader traits assumed to be static and unbending. While individual leaders may feel more comfortable in certain situations than in others, everyone will at one time or another face uncomfortable situations that can neither be changed nor ignored.

House's Path-Goal Contingency Theory

In 1971, R. J . House introduced the Path-Goal theory of leadership, which garnered a wide acceptance and following. House and his associates held that a leader's most vital role is to motivate followers. They advocated a system of clarifying paths to desired goals, enhanced by rewards. This theory arbitrarily addresses four leadership styles: directive, supportive, participative, and achievement oriented. House clearly dealt more with participation by followers than did Fiedler. In this respect, House put forth two major conclusions:

1. Participation is most appropriate when the follower's task is blurred or indefinite.
2. Participation is also most appropriate when followers require independence or tend to evince authoritarian traits.

Accordingly, House identified three contingencies facing the leader:

- The task
- Characteristics of subordinates
- The nature of the subordinate group

All of this emphasizes the leader's behavior as a source of satisfaction to subordinates.

Attention to these variables qualifies the Path-Goal theory as a premier contingency model of leadership.

The Vroom–Yetton Contingency Model

In 1973, a team led by Victor Vroom and Philip Yetton published what has been referred to as the normative contingency approach.

Like the work of Fiedler and House, it dealt with situational differences, focused on leaders' actions rather than their personalities, and embraced both follower qualities and task considerations. Its uniqueness is to be found in two broad arenas: first, in the amount and form of group participation in decision making; and second, in a more precisely defined concept of the term *situation*, to mean just exactly the problem/decision confronting the leader.

The researchers specified seven attributes through which a leader may evaluate and select the most effective decision-making process to follow:

A. The importance of the decision quality
B. The leader's information relevant to the problem
C. Extent to which the problem is structured
D. Importance of acceptance of decision by subordinates to effective implementation
E. Probability that the leader's decision will be accepted by subordinates
F. Congruence of organizational and subordinate goals
G   Conflict or disagreement among subordinates

Concerning the last of these, conflict, the model's advocates make four interesting observations:

1. Conflict among people increases the time that they will require to make joint decisions.
2. Conflict among people may polarize and be a source of divisiveness in subsequent relationships.
3. Conflict among people can lead to clearer thinking and better decisions.
4. Conflict among people is a sign that they should interact more (rather than less) frequently in an attempt to resolve their differences.

Although the first two of the above statements imply that conflict should be avoided, the third and fourth imply that conflict itself can be instructive and can be utilized.

The qualities of this model have to be something of a standard discipline in the academic treatment of leadership theory, especially with respect to the degree to which followers' acceptance is key to implementing leaders' decisions.

The Hersey–Blanchard Theory

A popular and easily understood contingency concept is the Hersey–Blanchard approach to situational leadership. This model singles out the followers' readiness, in terms of psychological maturity and job experience, as the prime contingency affecting the leader's decision to be either predominantly task oriented or more relations oriented.

A low level of maturity among subordinates requires a telling mode. As the level of the follower maturity rises, a transition should be made by the leader to selling, participating, and finally to delegating. Although this format is particularly apt in parent-child relationships, it also has relevance to other leadership situations.

A given leader might well adopt a delegating style with one group of followers and a selling or telling style with another, depending upon where they fall on the readiness continuum. Detractors of Hersey and Blanchard put forth these claims:

1. The analysis does not recognize that groups may have multiple maturities.
2. There is no provision in the theory for dealing with conflict or divisiveness.
3. There is no known research for validating their approach.

Bass on Task-Oriented vs. Relationship-Oriented Leadership

Piercing the finer points of the four foregoing contingency models, the director of the Center for Leadership Studies at the State University of New York at Binghamton, Dr. Bernard M. Bass, seems to have gotten to the core of it all in his revision of a time-honored leadership reference book, *Stogdill's Handbook of Leadership.*

What Bass sees as a common thread running through each of the contingency models is that, even though their proponents differ on many details, each acknowledges a leadership spectrum with a task orientation at one end and a relationship orientation at the other.

Task Orientation

Bass notes that task-oriented leaders, for example, have high concern for group goals and for production, are in need of achievement, are sometimes hard-driving persuaders, are often autocratic and usually aloof, and tend to be controlling supervisors.

Relationship Orientation

In the same manner, Bass presents the profile of the relationship-oriented leader as concerned with group maintenance, focused on people, supportive, interaction oriented, in need of affiliation, and expressly desirous of social ties.

Complications

Quite perceptively, Bass cites two more random possibilities that we find in leaders who are not all one way or the other:

1. There are those who seem to possess neither orientation and tend to drift from one mediocre performance and/or failure to another until they are relieved.
2. There are also "switch-hitters," like the benevolent autocrats who, though highly task oriented, are sufficiently enlightened to encourage participation in decision making in the interest of achieving better performance.

Contemporary Models

(Leader/Follower Dynamics)

Writers on leadership are so plentiful and so prolific that we doubt that anyone will ever be able to present the complete and current state of the leadership art. This is an elastic, restless, even seething subject, and the word itself, *leadership*, may well be the second most intangible word in our language. (This leaves room for each reader's nominee for first.)

For the purposes of this book, we shall endeavor to highlight some of the more significant contemporary models of leadership.

Focus on Followership

One development we see as favorable is the recent proliferation of concern for the follower and how best to achieve what has been termed followership. We think this perceptive trend has been long overdue.

In Part One, we were concerned with the conversion of followers to leaders and the importance of not taking refuge in the conventional excuses for letting opportunities for leadership go by default. None of the discussion that follows is intended either to diminish such initiative among our readers or in any way to interfere with the challenging process of leaving followership behind.

But leadership cannot exist for very long without strong followership, so it's probably just as well that some will opt to follow rather than lead. Indeed, collaboration between the two in a mutually responsive, interlocking relationship is the fulfilling fantasy of every leader. Yet, Dr. James L. Lundy, whose book *Lead, Follow, or Get Out of the Way* has been adopted for use in the classroom by more than a hundred colleges, has observed:

> Throughout many—or maybe even most—organizations, you can frequently hear the subordinates' lament. Although the exact phraseology may vary, the general message remains:
> WE THE UNINFORMED,
> WORKING FOR THE INACCESSIBLE,
> ARE DOING THE IMPOSSIBLE
> FOR THE UNGRATEFUL!

Dr. Lundy goes on to make the point that many followers do not feel involved, understood, or appreciated. Further, the better they are as followers, the more they expect to know about what is going on—and the more frustrated they are when they don't know. He then quotes a stress expert who claims that most of the jobholders in this country do not like their work. Other authorities claim that most married people don't like their spouses. Can this really mean that most of us neither want to go to work in the morning nor come home at night? What a testimonial for the need to have mutually responsive, interlocking relationships in our lives!

Historical Perspective: Traits Versus Situations

In the early studies of leadership, the primary focus was not on leader/follower dynamics, but rather on "leadership qualities"—the so-called trait theory. These studies emphasized the personal qualities of those occupying leadership roles. Other writers have referred to this approach as the grand theory, in contrast to the grounded theory, which came along later.

Another manifestation of the trait approach was the so-called great-man theory. Many observers saw human history as being shaped by the leadership of great men. Buss's revision of *Stogdill's Handbook of Leadership* puts it bluntly:

> Without Moses, the Jews would have remained in Egypt. Without Winston Churchill, the British would have given up in 1940. . . . The Russian Revolution would have taken a different course if Nikolai Lenin had been hanged by the Old Regime instead of exiled. For the romantic philoso-

phers, such as Friedrich Nietzsche, a sudden decision by a great man could alter the course of history (Thomas Jefferson's decision to purchase Louisiana, for example). . . . To William James (1880), the mutations of society were due to great men, who initiated movement and prevented others from leading society in another direction. The history of the world, according to James, is the history of Great Men. . . .

The individuals in every society possess different degrees of intelligence, energy, and moral force, and in whatever direction the masses may be influenced to go, they are always led by the superior few.

Early trait theorists explained leadership in terms of traits of personality and character. Bird compiled a list of seventy-nine such traits from twenty psychologically oriented studies. But the pure trait theory ultimately fell into disfavor, as critics concluded that both person and situation had to be included to explain the emergence of leadership.

Situationalism, the notion that the leader is the product of the surrounding circumstances, subsequently moved into favor. However, the controversy over which is more important, personality traits or the given situation, is an old one and still lives even today. As we saw in Study Four, those who downplay the situation are known as noncontingency theorists. They generally hold that theirs is the preferred approach to managing and/or leading because it is universal in its application.

Contingency theorists, on the other hand, hold that successful leadership must be adaptable to variable sets and subsets of contingencies, not the least of which is the followership variable.

The Personal-Situational Approach

There is an evident standoff here between the trait and situational theorists. Perhaps the best way of resolving it is to realize that neither traits nor situations by themselves are sufficient to account for all the different styles of leadership that have been observed. To quote *Stogdill's Handbook of Leadership* again:

James (1880) pointed out that the great man needs help— that his talents needed to fit with the situation. Ulysses S. Grant, for instance, was a continuing failure in private life before his emergence as the Union's great military commander, and he failed again as president. His rise to commanding general of the Army of the Potomac was delayed by the many political appointees who came before him and took turns displaying their ineptitude before exasperated President Lincoln turned to Grant. Grant's leadership in the Vicksburg campaign brought victory, despite the orders of his superior, General Halleck, to fall back toward New Orleans. But it was Grant's persistence, helped by congressmen, that overcame the inertia of the political appointment system, and this trait of persistence and confidence in his success marked the style with which he hammered out his military victories.

This analysis suggests that leadership should be regarded as a relationship among various persons in a given setting, rather than as a particular set of characteristics of the isolated individual.

Various behavioral theories have emphasized the receipt of rewards and/or the avoidance of punishment in the level of followership generated. The punishment/reward continuum is a strong influence upon the ultimate effectiveness of the leader, too, for they are rewarded or punished according to whether their efforts to lead have been successful or not.

Transactional vs. Transformational

Leaving aside psychoanalytical and psychohistorical theories, which certainly have their place in understanding certain egocentric political leaders, there is one overriding and useful criterion for the classification of most leadership styles. In the final analysis, most acts of leadership are either transactional or transformational.

Transactional approaches are those that offer either the promise of reward or the threat of discipline, depending upon followers' performance of specific and measurable tasks. Transformational acts of leadership are those that inspire and/or stimulate followers to join together in a mutually satisfying achievement of genuine consequence.

An article by Dr. Bernard M. Bass in the Winter 1990 *AMA Quarterly Review* offers a useful summary of characteristics of these two broad categories of leaders:

Transactional Leader

Contingent reward: Contracts exchange of rewards for effort . . . recognizes accomplishment

Management by
exception (active):   Watches and searches for deviations from rules and standards . . . takes corrective action

Management by
exception (passive):   Intervenes only if standards are not met

Laissez-faire: Abdicates responsibility . . . avoids making decisions

Transformational Leader

Charisma: Provides vision and sense of mission . . . instills pride . . . gains respect and trust

Inspiration: Communicates high expectations . . . uses symbols to focus efforts . . . expresses important purposes in simple ways

Stimulation: Promotes intelligence . . . rationality . . . and careful problem solving

Individualism: Gives personal attention . . . treats each follower separately . . . coaches . . . advises.

Bass gives a clear endorsement of the latter form: "Fostering transformational leadership through policies of recruitment, selection, promotion, training and development is likely to pay off in the health, well-being and effective performance of the organization."

What Bass is saying with conviction is that transformational leadership can and must be acquired. In a book he wrote with Avolio, Bass proclaimed, "Transformational leadership is closer to the prototype of leadership that people have in mind when they describe their ideal leader . . . a role model with which subordinates want to identify."

At this point, the question arises whether there is any rationale for a transformational leader ever to engage in transactional leadership. Our own view on this point is one born of instinct rather than of research. We certainly see nothing wrong in an established transformational leader resorting to the promise of rewards for the performance of followers, but we are doubtful about threats of penalty.

Philosophy of Choice

(Antifatalism)

Writing about philosophy, especially about a philosophy of life, can lead one into a quagmire of complex and often conflicting thought. Yet, ideas concerning leadership principles, skills, and applications are rooted within the long traditions of humankind. Through the ages, philosophers have addressed the major issues of life. Within their writings, especially those often characterized as religious writings, there is evidence of the eternal struggle between human likes and dislikes.

Life might be easier if we the people were physiologically or in some other way predisposed to do what is best for us. But if this were so, we would be robbed of perhaps life's most important freedom: the freedom of behavioral choice. Some prefer the term *self-determination*. For it is through choices that we learn about ourselves and expand our understanding of just who we are with respect to others as well as to our physical surroundings. Rather than existing as slaves of instinct or even of prior experience, as humans we can, through choice, become more and do more than we can now imagine.

Ancient Greeks

Even a cursory look back across human history shows how far we have come and at the same time how similar we are to our predecessors on this earth. In fact, the choices we have now are surprisingly similar to the choices that our forebears faced, though the context— the situation—in which we make these choices is of course different.

In the past, there were discussions of what we now address as leadership. We can see this when we read of the ancient gods and heroes, who are generally portrayed in a story as greater than mere mortals. Yet, these mythical characters possessed attributes that the storytellers and writers suggested that humans should emulate.

Unlike many journals today, which hold that anyone who leads must be without fault or failure, the ancients evaluated their heroes in terms of their overall contributions to humanity. Theseus, heralded for his athletic prowess and fighting ability, is also described as doing terrible things, such as raping Helen and Ariadne.

The noteworthy feats and exploits of the heroes were a result of their having chosen risky and daring actions. Most of these heroes were ultimately destroyed even though they seemed to be invincible. And, as it was their choices that led to victories, so, too, it was their choices that led to their destruction.

Zarathustra and the Iranian Religion

The philosophy of choice is freely espoused in the ancient eastern religions. The Persian sage Zarathustra developed a new direction in the religious thinking of his time. In this way, he decided what was the Good. "Man is called to follow the example of Ahura Mazda [the spirit of light and good], but he is free in his choice."

Israel and the Time of Kings and Prophets

It seems clear from reading about the history of Israel that choice was at the core of the people's religious life. On coming into the land of Canaan, the Israelites were directed by Yahweh, their God, to choose between "the Good" and "the Pagan" influences from the land they were entering. Some attempted to join the two influences (called syncretism). Jeroboam, the first leader of the northern kingdom of Israel, attempted to fuse the Canaanites' worship of golden calves with the Jews' worship of Yahweh. Of course, this violated Yahweh's prohibition against the worship of "graven images."

There was still a choice for the followers of Yahweh: they could obey the divine commandments, or they could reject them. Even the prophets, who were given a vision from Yahweh, had a choice of revealing or withholding what they had seen and/or heard.

Ancient Chinese Traditions

Over the centuries, the ancient Chinese religions evolved from a pre-occupation with creator gods toward a philosophy based on rationalism. The concept of the Tao—the mysterious and incomprehensible principle of universal order; the ineffable, ultimate origin that is immanent in all reality—helps to bridge the gap between religion and philosophy. The Tao produced three strong influences on ancient Chinese philosophical thought. These are the Heavenly Tao and the Earthly Tao, both of which were conceived of as contrasting forces (similar to the ying-yang principle), and the Tao of Man, which contains the code of conduct for humans. Consistent with the Tao of Man, humans choose among alternative actions as they strive toward the ideal.

Confucius developed his views within this philosophic context during a period of social injustice and anarchy. It is not surprising, therefore, that he and his students called for moral behavior (choice for the ideal) and that the highest good lay in leadership of the people through virtuous example rather than by decree. It is through this correct behavior that the leader obtains formidable moral power.

One final concept related to leadership that emerges from the ancient Chinese is the advice given to political and military leaders in the *Tao Te Ching* written by Lao Tzu. The best way for leaders to obtain power is not to put themselves into a position of authority or to unduly call attention to themselves. Instead, the leader should stay in the background, not be belligerent or impetuous, and remain nonviolent. Leaders increase their success when they exhibit the qualities of the androgyne (both male and female) ideal. Again, consistent with the ying-yang, leaders are to integrate what seem to be contradictory principles—or at least foster their coexistence. The freedom of choice is held paramount; coercion is wrong.

Traditional Leadership Characteristics

Looking at the history of mankind, there seem to be four different types of leaders. First, there were those with a sort of transcendent vision—prophets, holy men, seers, and the like. Second, many became leaders because they were able to fuse together two or more disparate groups or philosophies, producing a unity that had not previously existed. We can see this latter principle at work in the unification of the many different religious philosophies of the eastern religions and in the unification of the barons of feudal Europe into kingdoms.

A third factor seems to be a leader's propensity for instituting change. There is a commitment on the part of this type of leader to the outcome and purpose—the principles and priorities—not just to himself or herself and to those who follow.

The fourth type of leadership is often an outgrowth of the leader's view of the world. Those who see the world as basically positive tend to step out and take their place at the head of a movement for change. On the other hand, those who hold a negative or a diminished view of the world tend to retreat, seeking sanctuary rather than choice that leads to change.

In these four characteristics we can see the importance not only of choice but also of being able to address any situation in which one finds oneself. Acceptance of the hand one is dealt can lead to one of two things: Either play the hand, or fold and wait for a new hand to be dealt. Obviously, life is much more than playing cards. But the metaphor seems apt because the decision, the choice, is always the player's. And, ironically, many a hand has been played and has prevailed even when it was not the best hand at the table. The practice of wishing and waiting for a better hand loses many games. Even those who play and lose at least have the enjoyment of being part of the action.

There is another characteristic of leadership that is evident from taking a long look back across history—demagoguery, or playing on the followers' weaknesses and worst instincts. Distinguishing between the genuine leader and the demagogue is not always easy. Both advocate change. Both may unite different parties or opinions. Both may espouse some transcendent vision. And, both may be strongly committed to their vision of the future. But there is one thing that seems to separate the genuine leader from the demagogue. The leader never brings harsh punishment down on his or her detractors or opponents, trying to eliminate them. The demagogue is often ruthless; the genuine leader is benevolent.

Theological Treatment of Choice

Whatever we have learned in terms of the role of choice in the evolution of human behavior, our inquiry would be remiss not to get a sense of its theological validation or rejection. The world's major religions have very different views of self-determination and of fatalism.

Fatalism is both a doctrine and a state of mind. According to *Web-*

ster's Ninth New Collegiate Dictionary, it is "a doctrine that events are fixed in advance for all time in such a manner that human beings are powerless to change them." According to the *Encyclopaedia Britannica*, it is the attitude of mind that accepts whatever happens as having been bound or divinely decreed to happen. Similarly, antifatalism shall be construed for our purposes to mean self-determination, as both a doctrine and a state of mind.

Now let us examine the doctrines of some major world religions with regard to fatalism and self-determination.

Buddhism

The Buddhist view of predestination can be derived somewhat by induction. In the Pali canon, there is *sutta* (an exposition) on the doctrine that there are two extremes, both of which are repudiated: (1) the profitless life of indulgence in sensual pleasure and (2) the equally pointless way of self-torture. The clear inference here is that choice is assumed and that it shall be man's exclusive decision what path he shall follow.

Christianity

Since the birth and crucification of Christ, humanity is not at all a prisoner of fate; rather, since Jesus died for man's sins and then rose from the dead, Christians shall for all time be the beneficiaries of the doctrine that divinity does not shape man's ends. In Acts 2:17, the Apostle Peter said, ". . . young men shall see visions and your old men shall dream dreams." Our search and study disclosed no distinction in this area between Protestantism and Catholicism.

Hinduism

One of the central beliefs of Hindus is the transmigration of souls, or reincarnation in which the souls of humans (and animals) who die pass into new bodies as punishment or reward for the actions taken in the previous life. Thus people are endowed with freedom of choice to change their status.

Islam

The aim of education in Islam is to produce a good man. The prophet Muhammad said that Islam is built on five fundamentals: belief in God; prayer; fasting; pilgrimage to Mecca; and the giving of alms. While the Islamic Kodarites fought bravely in battle because they believed that Allah had foreordained their death or life, the more contemporary view is summed up by A. L. Tibawi in his book *Islamic Education:* "God has indeed predestined man's actions, but He had also created in him the power of responsibility to decide which course to follow. There is no fatalism in this, for fatalism implies acceptance of physical determinism . . ."

Judaism

One modern view of antifatalism is given by Kaufman Kohler in his book *Jewish Theology:* "The dignity and greatness of man depends largely upon his freedom, his power of self-determination. . . . He acts from free choice and conscious design and is able to change his mind at any moment, at any new evidence or even through whim. He is therefore responsible for his every act or omission . . ."

In each of these five major religions of the world, we have found that the philosophy of choice is strongly entrenched. In the words of the renowned psychologist Rollo May, "Real freedom is the ability to pause between stimulus and response and in that pause, choose."

PART 3

Six Leadership Principles

(The Basic Tenets on Which Leaders Can Rely)

> The strongest case for leadership is you don't have to do it all yourself.
>
> —Anonymous

Before there is practical application, there must be theoretical knowledge—at least if progress is to be made in a straight line rather than by starts, stops, and detours common to the trial-and-error process.

There are numerous principles of leadership that have been developed over the years. We have studied a great many of them and, for this section of the book, have taken those that made the most sense to us and synthesized *six principles* on which we hold that all great leadership is based. While these principles are by no means all-inclusive, to us they are indispensable, basic tenets all leaders must study and understand before they can go forward. Here they are:

1. The advantages of greater self-knowledge.
2. What leadership isn't.
3. Earning the leadership role.

4. The "G" and "P" words of motivation.
5. Planning is not all there is.
6. Relationship building.

But before we proceed with our presentation and analysis of these six fundamental leadership principles, some caveats seem in order:

First—many, many learned observations can be (and have been) made concerning what constitutes leadership; our chosen six are by no means preclusive—rather they are, to us, absolutely indispensable if one is to understand fully how to make it happen with a maximum chance of success.

Second—no amount of understanding of these proven principles alone can guarantee leadership success.

Third—the understanding of our six basic leadership skills is another essential ingredient.

Fourth—there is a literal chasm between merely understanding leadership skills and knowing how to apply them for long term success.

As we consider each of the six in succession, please observe how they have their roots in one or more of the pacesetting efforts that have gone before, as presented in Part Two.

PRINCIPLE 1

Leadership Begins With Greater Self-Knowledge

Since the leader/follower phenomenon, as suggested in the Preface, "can obviously involve as few as two individuals or as many as millions," what could be a more logical point of departure in your quest to lead than to examine objectively your own basic personality characteristics and normal behavioral tendencies? Indeed, you cannot realistically conceive of leading others, a task that clearly requires knowing and understanding them, without knowing and understanding yourself. In our search for greater self-knowledge, we shall explore the following topics:

- Self-knowledge over time
- Some basic personality characteristics
- Some normal behavioral tendencies
- Positioning yourself as to characteristics and tendencies
- Positioning yourself emotionally
- The ongoing challenge to self

Leadership is not a theoretical activity. It is based on real-life relationships with peers, with followers, and with yourself . . . for without truly knowing yourself, there is little chance you can get to know or establish a relationship with anyone else. The deepest understanding of the principles enunciated here will not be of much value unless they are put into practice with the cooperation of others.

Wisdom of the Ages

The benefits of greater self-knowledge have been long renowned. The ageless aphorism "Know thyself" was counted among the oracles, or precepts, of the ancient Greek gods. It was inscribed on the temple of Apollo at Delphi and regarded as divine wisdom.

Around 500 B.C. Confucius said, "The superior man will watch over himself when he is alone. He examines his heart that there may be nothing wrong there, and that he may have no cause of dissatisfaction with himself." "The most difficult thing in life is to know yourself," said Thales, a Greek philosopher who died in the year 546 B.C. at the age of 94. The Roman orator Marcus Tullius Cicero said, "The precept, 'KNOW THYSELF,' was not solely intended to obviate the pride of mankind; but likewise that we might understand our own worth."

"Of all knowledge, the wise and good seek most to know themselves," said William Shakespeare.

Johann Wolfgang von Goethe, eighteenth-century German poet and philosopher, said, "Self-knowledge is best learned, not by contemplation, but action. Strive to do your duty, and you will soon discover of what stuff you're made."

A less familiar English writer of the early nineteenth century, Edward George Bulwer, gave us this: "Know thyself, said the old philosophy—improve thyself, saith the new." In much less formal language, a veteran U.S. CEO, Richard Harrison of the Fleming Companies, more recently mused: "How I wish someone might have gotten me better acquainted with me before I took on this job; perhaps I could have filled in some of my missing skills in a much more orderly fashion than I subsequently did."

Indeed, self-knowledge remains indispensable for those who aspire to lead others. Awareness of your own character and knowing how best to use, improve, or compensate for your natural traits are clearly the leading criteria for being a successful leader. Conversely, those who attempt to lead without such knowledge will be fortunate to achieve mediocrity—and may fail completely without even knowing why. The problem is that only a few among us can knowingly say that they truly do have *thorough* and *precise* knowledge of their own personalities.

To be sure, most of us feel we know ourselves better than anyone else. This may create the illusion that we know all we need to know. If you believe that, please consider the following:

> "Can you really affirm that—thirty-one days ago—you could have reliably predicted your subsequent words and deeds during the past thirty days?"

Most of those to whom we have put this admittedly rhetorical question have acknowledged immediately that the things they said and the actions they took during that period were not nearly what they thought, ideally, they would have said and done. How is it that our perceptions of ourselves are so disparate from our real selves? Is it just too difficult to look ourselves directly in the eye? . . . or perhaps too painful? . . . or is it simply a matter of needing brighter lighting over our psychic mirrors? With more than twenty-five centuries of clearly expressed recognition by erudite scholars and intellectuals of the need for greater self-knowledge by all of us and especially those who lead, we strongly advocate it as the first of our six proven leadership principles.

Your Primary Personal Characteristics

It is not our purpose here to present a complete checklist of personality traits for you to use in making a better self-appraisal. Such an approach could of course consume volumes. Instead, our interest here is to provide you with a kind of springboard to facilitate a more thorough approach. Actually, there are four primary characteristics that merit consideration: your *interests*, your *abilities*, your *values*, and your *needs*. By analyzing these four areas, you can become much better acquainted with yourself; indeed, these just happen to be the same four templates that many job-search consultants focus upon as they perform their services.

But if you're still a bit uncomfortable, perhaps our favorite Norman Vincent Peale anecdote will be instructive here. "Dr. Peale was shaking hands after one of his speeches when he noticed a woman looking at him with a steady gaze. He made his way over to her and said, "Madam, did you want to speak to me?"

"Hello, Norman," the woman said, "don't you know me?"

"You have a familiar look", said Dr. Peale, "but I can't place you."

"I went to high school with you," she declared. "You know, you've really done very well with what little you had to start with."

"I thought that was quite a put-down," Dr. Peale recalled, "but then I got to thinking about it. You know, that's really what I've been speaking about and writing about all my life: Do the best you can with what little talent you've got, and you'll go far."

What a model philosophy, simple, sensible, and helpful. With this in mind, let's consider the four springboard characteristics we recommend using for greater self-knowledge.

Your Interests

Sure . . . you know your basic interests probably much better than anyone. But are you truly aware in any real depth of precisely what you would prefer to do, day-in and day-out, to make a living? Your ideal may be completely different from the job you have now and from others you've had in the past. Let's say you're still an undergraduate trying to decide what to choose for your major study and/or what elective studies to take. The Educational and Industrial Testing Service, in San Diego, features a Career Occupational Preference Service (COPS), in which the client is asked to respond to an array of 168 questions concerning on-the-job functions (from preparing meals to doing laboratory research, from designing furniture to conducting sales clinics). In this evaluation, the client indicates that he or she likes it very much, likes it moderately, dislikes it moderately, or dislikes it very much.

While the clients supply all the input, few know in advance exactly how their composite evaluation of interests is going to turn out. When the automated results are in, each client is presented with guidelines for self-development and productive growth. Most of them are surprised, and many of them, after some careful thought, redirect their lives accordingly. This procedure offers a clear lesson concerning the crucial need in most people for more introspection.

Your Abilities

The Educational and Industrial Testing Service also offers a Career Ability Placement Survey (CAPS), in which the client is provided with a digest of data about his or her abilities as an aid in career planning. Scores from a lengthy abilities questionnaire are evaluated in terms of strengths and weaknesses in mechanical reasoning, spatial relations, verbal reasoning, numerical ability, language usage, word knowledge, perceptive speed and accuracy, and manual speed and dexterity.

Your Values

In the same manner, the San Diego firm also offers a values profile study (COPES), in which the client's values are both identified and quantified as a final aid in career planning. Eight sets are presented with opposite value characteristics at the ends of each, as follows:

accepting	versus	investigative
carefree	versus	practical
conformity	versus	independence
supportive	versus	leadership
noncompulsive	versus	orderliness
privacy	versus	recognition
realistic	versus	aesthetic
self-concern	versus	social

The idea here again is for the client to answer a large number of questions. When plotted on a grid, the answers identify each person's major and minor values on the eight sets and these, in turn, suggest career clusters for the client's consideration, with an accompanying educational direction at the college level.

Your Needs

We reject the notion that even one individual—let alone entire groups of individuals—can be conveniently labeled according to his or her basic needs and/or tendencies and neatly relegated to certain predictable behavioral patterns to the exclusion of all others for a lifetime. What a drab existence this would be for anyone! What we do believe instead is that, for example, some of us are more (or less) assertive than others; similarly, we each tend much of the time to be more (or less) oriented to the *task* at hand rather than the *people* involved in the process. David C. McClelland held that two of the most powerful and basic needs within each of us—in varying degrees, of course, are the need for achievement (*N* Achievement) and the need for power (*N* Power).

In the 1950s, a successful young insurance agent, Larry Wilson, got together with a team of psychologists and management consultants and formed the Wilson Learning Company. They soon introduced what became known as the Wilson Personality Grid (Figure 2). Since that time, it has been the touchstone of the firm's motivational and sales training programs presented to some of the nation's leading corporate executives.

We commend it to anyone who wishes to organize his or her self-knowledge around a durable format which, in turn, can also serve as a template for identifying basic tendencies in others.

The grid and its four quadrants are formed by a vertical axis with OBJECTIVE (or task orientation) at the top and SUBJECTIVE (or people orientation) at the bottom (a direct tie to McClelland's *N* Achieve-

Figure 2.   The Wilson Personality Grid.

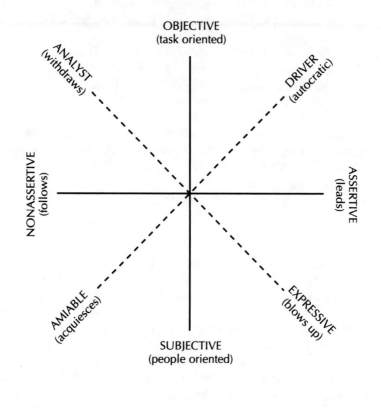

I. Never Tries	II. Sometimes Tries	III. Usually Tries	IV. Always Tries
Versatility Scale			

Source: Larry Wilson, *Personality Grid—Managing Interpersonal Relationships,* © 1978. All rights reserved. Reprinted by permission of Wilson Learning Corporation.

ment) and a horizontal axis with ASSERTIVE on the right and NONAS-
SERTIVE on the left (a direct tie to McClelland's *N* Power).

But An Acorn Can Only Become an Oak Tree

It is the natural tendency of an acorn to grow into a stately oak, not
an elm, a maple, or a hickory. But human beings are more complex
organisms than trees. Nobody is born with all of the ready-made
characteristics of a successful chief executive officer, the "stately oak"
of the business world. Such traits and skills can be learned. And that
is what this book is all about. Of course, people vary with respect to
their "task" versus "people" orientation and their relative "assertive-
ness." And that is what the Wilson Personality Grid is all about.

1. (Upper right) the assertive task-oriented type—the *driver*
2. (Lower right) the assertive people-oriented type—the *expressive*
3. (Lower left) the nonassertive people-oriented type—the *amiable*
4. (Upper left) the nonassertive task-oriented type—the *analyst*

Larry Wilson claims that the best way to plot a person's position
on the grid is to ask a hundred questions of five of the person's
friends (other than family). Of course, it's rare to have the opportunity to interrogate five friends of each individual you need to know
well. Fortunately, some reasonably reliable alternatives are available.
By becoming aware of what makes an individual tick, you can gain
invaluable insight on how to predict behavior and deal with it.

Wilson recommends studying people's backup systems, that is,
how they behave when challenged or thwarted. He has found that:

The driver becomes autocratic.
The expressive blows up.
The amiable acquiesces.
The analyst withdraws.

The Versatility Scale

Unlike the acorn-oak, human beings have the capacity to modify and
consciously change behavior to a given situation. The versatility scale
below the grid in Figure 2 presents four stages of proficiency in terms

of at least making an effort. Whatever the results may be when one endeavors to become more versatile, the scale itself is an invitation to risk trying to be flexible in return for the occasional triumph.

For example, perceptive drivers have learned to be less assertive on occasions when maintaining an autocratic attitude would only delay or perhaps prevent a satisfactory solution. Enlightened analysts have found that a more expressive dialogue can sometimes do wonders toward a solution when withdrawal would only impede or entirely defeat further progress. However difficult it may be for expressives to resist blowing up when a situation seems completely hopeless, mature people know that a more composed and patient analytical attitude can occasionally open up a new, more productive approach. Similarly, many well-adjusted amiables have learned how important it can be at times to be more assertive in pursuit of the task rather than remain preoccupied with seeking the approval of others involved in the process.

Not everyone finds it possible to be versatile. Indeed, many who made "all their mistakes in the same field" have ultimately became recognized as "experts." Some drivers, expressives, amiables, and analysts can persist along their paths of greatest tendency and do reasonably well. However, those who learn to know themselves well enough so that they realize who they really are, where they are clearly deficient, and how they can become more versatile in dealing with others will soon find that their levels of effectiveness can be enhanced enormously.

As you become more versatile, you will be preoccupied with new challenges, new skills, and—sure—a few defeats as you tackle exciting new opportunities far beyond your former reach. You may never make "expert," but who cares?

Your Quadrant on the Grid?

Perhaps you already know. For those who don't—and who don't have Larry Wilson to ask five of your close friends a "hundred confidential personality questions"—we present an abbreviated, private do-it-yourself assessment in Figure 3. This is not a test—there are no incorrect answers—but a simple, painless way to find out where you stand on the Wilson Personality Grid. Do it now.

For still more penetrating self-knowledge, see Figure 4, which shows some distinctive characteristics of the four quadrant personalities along with some "role models" for each type.

Figure 3. Do-it-yourself assessment of your position on the Wilson Personality Grid.

```
                        1
                        2
                        3
      6    5    4          3    2    1
                        4
                        5
                        6
```

With as little hesitation as possible, please indicate whether the following state-ments are *generally* true or *generally* false concerning your own personal attitudes (there are no wrong answers):

	True	False
Generally, I would rather follow than lead.		
I welcome assistance in making my choice of national political candidates.		
I seem to have some bossy friends, but I like them anyway.		
I often need help with my career decisions.		
I usually try to follow current clothing styles.		
I rarely make financial decisions alone.		
TOTAL		

Please circle the number of true answers on the horizontal line on the grid above (treat a "zero" as a "one").

	True	False
I tend to make friends quite easily.		
I enjoy being impulsive once in a while.		
I depend upon intuition more than facts when weighing difficult decisions.		
Upon meeting new people, I'm inclined to trust them until they prove untrustworthy.		
Others do not think I am distant.		
I am more people oriented than task oriented.		
TOTAL		

Please circle the number of your true answers on the vertical line on the grid above (treat a "zero" as a "one"). Then connect the circles with two lines at a right angle to locate your quadrant.

Your Emotional Mix

On each of our treks through life's briar patch of successes and fail-ures, who among us can claim that our emotions have had no effect?

Figure 4. Characteristics of the four quadrants of the Wilson Personality Grid.

Categories	I. Driver	II. Expressive	III. Amiable	IV. Analyst
Tendency:	Controlling Dictatorial Cool	Creative Energetic Warm	Agreeable Friendly Caring	Attentive Systematic Organized
Backup System:	Autocratic Arrogant	Blows up Loses control	Acquiesces Submits	Withdraws Returns
Needs:	Control Power	Popularity Recognition	Security Belonging	Controlled Work and orderly tasks
Reward:	They feel superior and expect people to submit	They like to be the center of attention	They prefer never to take risks	They are usually well prepared
Strengths:	Decisive Self-confident	Persuasive Optimistic	Likable Team player	Accurate Precise
Weaknesses:	Intimidates and alienates others	Egotistical, lacks follow-through	Indecisive, wastes time	Stubborn, aloof, and unimaginative
How to Deal With:	Support their decisions and be businesslike	Use flexibility and let them express themselves	Be casual and sincere; do not rush	Go step by step, with facts and logic
Role Models:	J. R. Ewing	Johnny Carson	Bob Newhart	Coach Tom Osborne
	Margaret Thatcher	Liza Minelli	June Cleaver	Angela Lansbury

Once again, we ask you to invest a few minutes in a final self-analysis, in order to round out this vital segment of your self-knowledge, your emotional mix (please see Figure 5).

On the honor system, after you have completed Figure 5, then and only then complete your emotional self-assessment by referring to the box below.

A Final Conduit

Self-knowledge is not a static undertaking. Throughout the remainder of this book, you will be offered various approaches to cultivating your leadership talents. To the extent these talents are enhanced, your responses to our various exercises are going to undergo dynamic change.

What we're saying here is that no one remains the same for long—especially one who is determined to mature as a leader. We therefore urge our readers to resolve to reconsider each of this book's tests and exercises six months hence. The resulting six-month contrast can not only be significant in terms of one's individual growth, but also clear confirmation of how rewarding leadership challenges and resulting changes can be.

Former NBC commentator Ellerbee has opined that: "There are really only two kinds of change—those we choose and those that choose us." Concerning this pearl, we suggest that it is imperative to maintain a strong ratio in favor of the former. Choosing change is one of the purest forms of personal leadership, which can only come after enlightened *self-knowledge*.

PERSONAL SCORING AND SUMMARY

(Do not read this part until you have completed Figure 5.)

According to Dr. Eugene J. Benge, the creator of this personality assessment, the items labeled with the letters D, E, or F are valuable clues to a person's emotional mix, as follows:

Four or more D items suggest the possible presence of HATE.
Four or more E items suggest the possible presence of FEAR.
Four or more F items suggest the possible presence of GUILT.

It's important not to "cheat" on these self-assessments. Successful people find out the truth and then deal with it. For instance, if you

Figure 5   Your emotional mix (a self-analysis).

Check the 30 items which best apply to you (try hard for 30).

1D	I'm very impatient	31D	Resent life's injustices
2E	Evade responsibility when I can	32E	Afraid of some tame animals
3F	Failed in most of my ambitions	33F	Neglected my parents
4A	Have faith in people	34A	I have great patience
5B	My job is secure	35B	Optimistic about future health
6C	I'm an honest person	36C	I can't consciously hurt anyone
7D	Often use sarcasm	37D	Afraid I have a "short fuse"
8E	Crowds frighten me	38E	Feel insecure in my job
9F	Have some sex guilt	39F	Doubt the value of prayer
10A	Envy virtually no one	40A	Rarely if ever use sarcasm
11B	Equal to life's problems	41B	Parents were loving
12C	Made good work progress	42C	Achieved many of my goals
13D	People can't be trusted	43D	Folks say I'm intolerant
14E	Inadequate; feel inferior	44E	Some people intimidate me
15F	Wasted educational opportunities	45F	Have done some dishonest things
16A	Most things work for the best	46A	Rarely play "practical jokes"
17B	Do not fear death	47B	Accept responsibility
18C	Prayer brings me comfort	48C	Thoughtful of my parents
19D	Play mean tricks on people	49D	Envy many people
20E	Health outlook is poor	50E	Thought of death scares me
21F	Have been unjust to someone	51F	Made little work progress
22A	Readily forgive others	52A	I take frustration in stride
23B	Not afraid of anyone	53B	Like most tame animals
24C	Have met parents' expectations	54C	Seized educational opportunities
25D	Brood over injustices to me	55D	Hold grudges against some folks
26E	Easily swayed by others	56E	Parents hostile toward me
27F	Ignore others' misfortunes	57F	Failed my parents' hopes for me
28A	Tolerate other races or religions	58A	Throw off feelings of injustice
29B	Form my own firm opinions	59B	Enjoy crowds
30C	No guilt as to sex	60C	Help others less fortunate

Source: Eugene J. Benge, Ph.D. *How To Use Your Physical and Emotional Ability to Overcome Your Problems and Realize Your Goals* (Homewood, Ill.: Business ONE Irwin, 1977), p. 172.

checked four or more such items, you are to be commended for your honesty with yourself—a high character trait not shared by all. We therefore have no doubt that you will also find the wisdom and determination to follow the advice of another great emotional researcher, Dr. Raymond Pearl of Johns Hopkins University, who contends that:

"THE MOST RELIABLE ROUTE TO LONGEVITY AND PEACE OF MIND IS TO LOCK OUT OF YOUR LIFE THE UNHOLY TRINITY: HATE, FEAR, AND GUILT IN ANY FORM."

PRINCIPLE 2

Leadership Is Not Simply Good Management

Understanding the Differences

With only a few exceptions, the 272 accredited colleges of business in this country tend to organize their curricula around the basic functional areas of business, such disciplines as accounting, business law, business communications, economics, finance, marketing, and management. Of all these specialties, it is generally the management division that garners the greatest enrollment of students.

Webster's Ninth New Collegiate Dictionary defines a manager as "one who conducts or supervises something (as a business)," whereas the same source defines a leader as "one that exercises paramount but responsible authority." In this section, we shall elaborate upon some of the ways in which the role of responsible leadership is distinguishable from mere supervision and management. This is not to imply that managing tends to be irresponsible—far from it—even though the word *responsible* only found its way into one of the definitions in the dictionary and not the other.

We feel strongly that understanding the differences between management and leadership is crucial to becoming an enlightened leader; it ranks second only to self-knowledge among our six principles of leadership.

Before we begin our own identification of the differences, we first cite fairly recent and conflicting statements by authorities on the subject, and then contrast the characteristics of management and of leadership—all calculated to impart what we conclude "leadership isn't."

A High-Level Clash

In their 1982 book *In Search of Excellence,* Tom Peters and Bob Waterman called for more leaders and fewer managers:

> Many of today's managers—MBA trained and the like—may be a little bit too smart for their own good . . . but the people who lead the excellent companies are a bit simplistic . . . only those simplistic people—like Watson, Hewlett, Packard, Kroc, Mars, Olsen, McPherson, Marriott, Procter, Gamble, Johnson—stayed simplistic. And their companies have remained remarkably successful.

Three years later, in *A Passion for Excellence,* Peters and Nancy Austin declared that "the word *managing* should be discarded altogether." They also reported that "Warren Bennis, a major figure in the current rethinking process, says, 'American organizations have been overmanaged and underled.'"

On the other hand, Harold Geneen, the man who built ITT into a major worldwide conglomerate, believed that "leadership is purely subjective, difficult to define and virtually impossible to measure objectively." Many among the ranks of management faculties have stated that leadership is merely a tool that managers may, or may not, elect to use. (This sentiment, we fear, persists today in some quarters.) The headline of a recent advertisement by United Technologies in a trade journal read: "Let's get rid of management." It went on to say:

> Whoever heard of a world manager? World leader? . . . yes. Educational leader, political leader, religious leader, scout leader, community leader, labor leader, business leader . . . they lead; they don't manage. The carrot wins over the stick. Ask your horse—you can lead your horse to water, but you can't manage him to drink.

It is easy to get bogged down in semantics and to lose sight of the real issue, which is simply to ensure that those in charge will inspire a maximum productive effort from everyone involved. Thus, *fostering growth in others* is what those in charge should be doing. And that phenomenon, when it happens, is most often the result of a correct assessment of (1) the difficulty of the task and (2) the experience of the group. Only after making such an assessment can those in charge apply the proper mix of what we might call *managerial leadership*.

Rear Admiral Grace Hopper of the U.S. Navy said it best in just four words:

MANAGE THINGS . . . LEAD PEOPLE.

A useful corollary might be:

MANAGE YOURSELF . . . LEAD OTHERS!

We believe the implications of these simple phrases are enormous.

That Which Is, Is . . . That Which Isn't, Isn't

On which side are you more comfortable when you're in charge?

Management	*versus*	*Leadership*
restricting		enabling
controlling		freeing
playing safe		risking
molding		releasing
forcing		enhancing
regimenting		challenging
stifling		participating
rigid		flexible
autocratic		democratic
consistent		predictable
Managers do things right.		*Leaders do right things.* *

If you're not completely certain about your comfort level on one side or the other, see Figure 6. Take a few moments to give your *first-impression* responses to the twenty-one pairs of choices (arranged in three groups). By determining your rating, you may gain invaluable

*Adapted from Warren Bennis and Burt Nanus, *Leaders* (New York: Harper & Row, 1985).

insight into your management-oriented tendencies as opposed to your leadership-oriented tendencies.

More than that, you can also identify some highly useful directions for self-development. Thus, an individual with an ABC rating— "realistic, focused, and organized"—might well undertake to become at times more "visionary, caring, and adaptable," the earmarks of the XYZ rating. In other words, whatever the rating, one should have a look at the opposite letter values for clues to achieving a more balanced outlook.

The Ideal Mix

There is a powerful case to be made for achieving a rating near the center (AYC, XBC, AYZ, XBZ). In fact, managerial leadership, an integration of all six characteristics to fit the individual situation, may well offer the best opportunity for success at the helm. The creator of the concept in Figure 6, a widely read management consultant named Craig R. Hickman, gave strong support to this thesis in his book *Mind of a Manager, Soul of a Leader*.

> The words "manager" and "leader" are metaphors representing two opposite ends of a continuum. "Manager" tends to signify the more analytical, structured, controlled, deliberate, and orderly end of the continuum, while "leader" tends to occupy the more experimental, visionary, flexible, uncontrolled, and creative end. Given these fairly universal metaphors of contrasting organizational behavior, I like to think of the prototypical manager as the person who brings the thoughts of the mind to bear on daily organizational problems. In contrast, the leader brings the feelings of the soul to bear on those same problems. Certainly, managers and leaders both have minds and souls, but they each tend to emphasize one over the other as they function in organizations. The mind represents the analytical, calculating, structuring, and ordering side of tasks and organizations. The soul, on the other hand, represents the visionary, passionate, creative, and flexible side. . . .

The inference from the title of Hickman's book is that only managers have minds and only leaders have souls. This statement may provoke some disagreement, but its very provocativeness makes the case for judiciously blending the two sets of characteristics.

Figure 6. Your managerial leadership tendency (a brief self-portrait).

Without dwelling too heavily on any one pair of characteristics below, circle the letter to the *left* of the description which more closely identifies you most of the time. After considering each characteristic objectively, quickly indicate your *first impression*. (There are no incorrect answers.)

A — You prefer dealing with facts.
A — You are focused on the present.
A — You would like to build something.
A — You think you are practical.
A — You prefer the proven approach.
A — Most others say you are conventional.
A — You prefer to avoid risk.

TOTAL As _____

B — Most of your decisions are based on thoughts.
B — You are usually thorough.
B — You can be very analytical.
B — You attribute your successes mostly to logic and reason.
B — You attribute your failures mostly to lack of experience.
B — Most others say you are tough.
B — You prefer working alone.

TOTAL Bs _____

X — You prefer dealing with ideas.
X — You are focused on the future.
X — You would like to create something.
X — You think you are conceptual.
X — You prefer the challenge.
X — Most others say you are innovative.
X — You are not uncomfortable with risk.

TOTAL Xs _____

Y — Most of your decisions are based on feelings.
Y — You are sometimes impulsive.
Y — You sometimes act on instinct.
Y — You attribute your successes mostly to intuition and sensing.
Y — You attribute your failures mostly to lack of determination.
Y — Most others say you are easygoing.
Y — You prefer working with people.

TOTAL Ys _____

C — You like to make plans.
C — Unfinished tasks make you uncomfortable.
C — You abide by standards.
C — You make things happen.
C — You rarely change your mind.
C — Most others say you are set in your ways.
C — Consistency pays.

TOTAL Cs _____

Z — You prefer spontaneity.
Z — You don't mind letting things ripen.
Z — You question some of the rules.
Z — You let things happen.
Z — Changing your mind doesn't bother you.
Z — Most others say you are pliable.
Z — Flexibility pays.

TOTAL Zs _____

Thank you. Now, determine your (three-letter) tendency rating by combining the higher total of each of the three pairs (i.e., A or X; B or Y; C or Z).

Your rating: _____

Next, find your rating among the eight possibilities on the managerial leadership scale below.

Managerial Leadership Scale

Management oriented							Leadership oriented
ABC	ABZ	AYC	XBC	AYZ	XBZ	XYC	XYZ
realistic	realistic	realistic	visionary	realistic	visionary	visionary	visionary
focused	focused	caring	focused	caring	focused	caring	caring
organized	adaptable	organized	organized	adaptable	adaptable	organized	adaptable

An original adaptation of a concept presented by Craig R. Hickman, *Mind of A Manager, Soul of a Leader* (New York: John Wiley, 1990). Reprinted by permission of John Wiley & Sons, Inc.

Hickman adds still another dimension from the organizational point of view when he says, "There is a time for iron-willed polarizing, and there is a time for flexible compromising. If you only know how to compromise, you miss the tonic effect of polarizing; if you only know how to polarize, you miss those opportunities where a little bending could save the day."

Upon reflection, we have known effective managers who were not renowned for their compromising nature and successful leaders who worked exceedingly hard to avoid polarization within their ranks.

What we're recommending here is that you develop an aroused consciousness not only of where you tend to be on the manager-leader continuum, but also of the opportunities for individual growth and enhanced effectiveness that are uncovered in striving for the ideal—managerial leader.

A Whole New Dimension—Rating the Boss

How easy it is for managerial leaders to take comfort in their own mix of the characteristics that constitute the manager-leader continuum. One would think that an adroit orchestration of these six traits—realistic (A), focused (B), organized (C), visionary (X), caring (Y), and adaptable (Z)—depending upon situational circumstances, would serve one well in the pursuit of effective leadership. However, the fact is that the leader/employer is all too often far out of touch with the real sentiments of the follower/employee.

Conversely, like it or not, subordinates are constantly evaluating the attributes and shortcomings of the boss. Indeed, the relatively recent phenomenon in American business of subordinate appraisal has introduced a whole new dimension to the definition of leadership: In the eyes of most employees, the trait of caring outweighs by far all the others combined. In the words of James F. Hind in his book *The Heart and Soul of Effective Management:*

"People want to know how much you care before they care how much you know."

Further, caring is the key to maintaining morale within a group of employees. Yet, some executives we have known—even some who have feared low morale more than the reaction of shareholders to the dreaded lower earnings report—have not been able to understand caring. It just wasn't in them. Letter B on the continuum, "focused," would describe them every time.

Fear of bad morale even more than a down quarter in earnings is entirely legitimate. After all, lower earnings can be raised, but a decline in morale is usually a chronic problem that can linger for years. Once employees find out that management doesn't care, they may never again hold their bosses in esteem.

Those managers who choose to experiment with some form of subordinate appraisal merely to let employees "blow off a little steam" are abusing an invaluable tool for learning how their styles of managerial leadership are perceived and thus may not learn when necessary and timely changes can be made in that style in order for them to do a better job.

But, those executives who are willing to stick their necks out and implement a program of manager evaluation will benefit from the work of Professor Henry Mintzberg at McGill University in Montreal. His model includes ten criteria well suited for subordinate supervisory appraisal of a chief executive as:

- Leader
- Information disseminator
- Crisis handler
- Entrepreneur
- Resource allocator
- Environmental monitor
- Liaison
- Negotiator
- Spokesman
- Organizational representative

Professor Mintzberg suggests six graduated performance rankings for each quality, so that each manager is rated on a scale of 0 to 5, as follows:

Not at all—0
To a very limited extent—1
To a limited extent—2
To a moderate extent—3
To a fairly large extent—4
To a great extent—5

Of course, subordinate appraisal has its detractors. There are basically six major concerns:

1. Managers will focus on just trying to please subordinates.
2. The authority of the manager will be undermined.
3. Subordinates are not qualified to rate managerial performance.
4. Some seasoned managers will not stand for subordinate appraisals and will quit their jobs.
5. Some subordinates may deliberately downgrade the manager if they have been in any way abused in the past.
6. Some subordinates will be reluctant to tell the truth.

Management Obsolescence

Another way in which managers differ from leaders is that, over time, managers become obsolete, locked as they are into the old established methods, while leaders continue to grow as they confront new challenges and tasks. Our fellow Oklahoman, Robert Randolph, in his acclaimed book *Planagement*, laid out fifteen ways in which managers become ineffective and obsolete:

1. Their predictions of the future are based only on past experiences, and they manage momentum, not potential. They have run out of challenges and are frustrated because they have not been able to establish new and self-actualizing objectives.
2. They concentrate on weaknesses rather than strengths—they know what's wrong, not what's right—and their negative attitude makes them pessimists who see the difficulty in every opportunity rather than the opportunity in every difficulty. They are also defensive and unable to identify a direction for themselves that would improve their unhappy situation.
3. They make the simple seem complex, attempt to make themselves indispensable, and won't delegate authority to others.
4. They judge people by their traits and actions rather than by the results they obtain. They are inclined to emphasize know-who much more than know-how.
5. They rely on numbers and data rather than on people. Since they don't believe in people (usually they think the behavioral sciences are a lot of "academic nonsense"), they are more exploiters than builders. They trust no one and consider personal survival the most important law.
6. They are poor communicators and thus are constantly misunderstood. They are anxious talkers and poor listeners.

7. They are afraid of enthusiasm and extensively use sarcasm or cynicism to dampen it. They take credit but rarely give it, and they are usually against an idea that was "not invented here."

8. They pride themselves on getting the best deal rather than a fair deal. They know more answers than questions, and they depend on the right to hire and fire for their authority rather than on earned privilege.

9. They manipulate people and pride themselves on being excellent politicians. The other guy is the competition who may be after his job, so it becomes a business game to "get him first."

10. They frequently procrastinate rather than make decisions they will be held responsible for.

11. They are more conscious of position and activity than of direction and results. The *how* is emphasized, not the *why*.

12. Frequently, their approach is to establish a budget first, and then develop the plan the budget is supposed to support. Functional thinking is more pronounced than profit thinking.

13. They resist change, new ideas, and orderly procedures and tend to avoid establishing proper policies, procedures, and paperwork.

14. They are dictatorial and inflexible. They dislike the participative management approach and are extremely protective of their prerogatives. To them, it is more important to establish a point than to find the truth or the best answer. They manage by *their* objectives—and all others are subordinate.

15. These managers do not lead by example; their philosophy is, "Do as I say, not as I do." They are organized, escapist, and undisciplined. They follow no physical fitness program and rarely feel better than adequate. They lack direction and priorities, and their judgments depend almost entirely on past experience, intuition, and emotion rather than on a balance between these important elements and a logical and factual approach.

Whether or not a business executive becomes obsolete is basically up to each individual and his or her dedication to the ever-changing, always demanding tasks involved in leadership. No occupation or profession is free from risks in this area. Even professional window washers must strive constantly to enhance their relative value in the marketplace or, you can bet on it, some kind of window washing machine will take their place. We all must hone our skills regularly if we are to avoid obsolescence. The great classical pianist Jan Paderewski embraced the concept well: "If I miss one day of practice, I can tell it in my playing. If I miss two days in succession, my critics can tell it. If I miss a week, my audience can tell."

As a matter of principle, the enlightened leaders know that their techniques may not necessarily be all bad . . . they may just be obsolete. Such leaders also know that—once having accepted the mantle of leadership—the ancient "philosopher king" concept of Socrates and Plato is a far better course and one that has thoroughly survived the test of time (see Part Two, Study 1).

Leadership Must Be Earned

Inertia of Rest

The word *inertia* perhaps brings memories of Physics 101 and the basic scientific concept that all matter tends to remain at rest, if at rest; or, if moving, to keep moving in the same direction. More succinctly, inertia of rest is defined simply as the disinclination to move or act.

People are also subject to the laws of physics. It takes some effort to break inertia, to get moving, physically or mentally. Those who have never led anything are, of course, at rest insofar as leadership is concerned; and the longer they remain inert vis-à-vis leadership, the more difficult it will be for them to become motivated to lead.

Why Followers Follow

In general, followers fall into three general categories:

1. Those who are disinclined to act; having long been at rest as followers, they are comfortable to remain there.
2. Those who might be inclined to lead, except for their devotion to one or more of the mythical excuses presented in Part One.
3. Those who simply do not know—and, for the most part, don't much care—why they are content to follow.

We strongly suspect that the third segment is exceedingly large. The typical response in this group is: "I really don't know why I have followed my various leaders. . . . I just know it [leadership] when I see it."

The Achievement Criterion for You

How do followers "know" leadership when they "see" it? More to our point, why have you followed your leaders? For instance, have you ever followed someone blindly before they had achieved anything? Of course not—it just doesn't happen that way. Was not your willingness to follow because your chosen leader had demonstrated one or more successes?

To attract followers—indeed, for them to "know it when they see it"—a leader must have a record of achievement on some noticeable level.

IF YOU WOULD LEAD, YOU TOO MUST BEGIN BY BUILDING A RECORD OF ACHIEVEMENT—EVEN IF SOME OF YOUR EARLY GOALS ARE RELATIVELY EASY AT FIRST AND EVEN IF SOME ARE UNATTAINED.

Even great leaders are not always successful. No one can "bat a thousand!"

Achievement is the *criterion* for attracting followers . . . indeed, the key to earning the leader's mantle . . . but it need not be at a lofty level, and the success record need not be perfect.

The Bottom Line

John Naisbitt put it succinctly when he concluded a two-day leadership symposium at the University of Oklahoma by saying:

My bottom line on all of this leadership business is kind of plain. A leader must have at least two things . . . and, sometimes, a third thing.

First, you can't be a leader without attracting followers;

Second, you gotta have somewhere to take them . . . a clear destination; and

Third, but only when it's truly appropriate, you need a timetable.

To understand when a timetable may or may not be indicated, we shall cite a couple of presidential anecdotes:

- In 1961, soon after John Fitzgerald Kennedy took office, he proclaimed, in effect, "Follow me—and we shall land a man on the moon before the end of this decade." Such a pronouncement would have been empty without the time frame.
- In 1990, George Herbert Walker Bush declared, in effect: "Follow me—and we shall remove the Iraqi aggressor from Kuwait." Such a pronouncement would have been irresponsible with a deadline, without a clearer mandate from the United Nations, and until troop strength was in place to make it happen, if necessary.

Back to your own bottom line. We implore you to keep building a success record with the knowledge that early, consistent achievement is the essential criterion for earning a following.

How to Make It Happen

In closing this discussion of achievement and its place in the leadership process, we offer two anecdotes that should be useful memory pegs as you go about the task of making it happen. Both stories are related by James C. Humes in his book *Speaker's Treasure of Ancedotes About the Famous*.

The first reinforces the necessity of establishing a record of achievement. When Charles M. Schwab had not yet become a great industrialist in his own right, he worked for Andrew Carnegie. The little Scotsman taught him the hard lesson of the commercial world, that one day's laurels are of little use on the next. "All records broken yesterday," Schwab once wired to his chief; in reply to which Carnegie telegraphed, "But what have you done today?"

The second is a reminder of who will be watching: Dr. Johnson and his friend Boswell were at the Drury Lane Theatre together watching the great actor David Garrick. Boswell said to Johnson, "Garrick is not himself tonight," and the great man replied, "No."

All at once, Garrick commenced to act superbly, and Boswell remarked, "Do you notice how he has changed and changed for the better?"

"Yes," said the old sage, "and did you notice at what point he changed? He took a higher style when Edmund Burke came into the theater."

Each of us tends to do our best when we know we're being watched by the right people. Remember, as you set out to earn leadership through achievement, that your future followers will be watching.

Motivation Begins With the "G" Word—Goal— and Ends With the "P" Word—Participation

Many American business executives lack a basic understanding of motivation. This was illustrated in a research study led by Professor Kenneth Kovak of the University of Maryland. After Kovak and his team reached a consensus concerning the ten most significant motivating factors at work in American business today, they presented the list of factors to several thousand business executives with the request to rank them from one to ten in the order believed to be most influential among the executives' employees. Simultaneously, the same request was made of the employees of the same businesses. The aggregate results were collated with fascinating results, as follows:

Ranking by Employers	*Ranking by Employees*
1. Money	1. Appreciation
2. Job security	2. Being an insider
3. Chance for promotion	3. Personal sympathy
4. Work conditions	4. Job security
5. Interesting work	5. Money
6. Organizational loyalty	6. Interesting work
7. Tactful disciplining	7. Chance for promotion
8. Appreciation	8. Organizational loyalty
9. Personal sympathy	9. Work conditions
10. Being an insider	10. Tactful disciplining

This survey provided a sad commentary on the perceptions of employers. How could bosses be so wide of the mark as to rank 8, 9, and 10 the top three motivating factors named by the employees! Given the growing competition from abroad, American business should be highly motivated to learn more about what really gets results among its people.

Here's the point . . . and it's a powerful one: The top three of the employees' motivators are all well within the control of the employers to deliver. Conveying appreciation . . . making the staff feel like insiders . . . and projecting an attitude of sympathy for personal problems requires only a more enlightened use of time by the supervisor, not a new allocation of dollars. Perhaps the occasional seminar, a Christmas week breakfast, a series of luncheons will require some cash outlay. But it's a fact that these three top motivators are not managed best by throwing dollars at them. What it obviously comes down to is the leadership quality of caring (already discussed under Principle 2). And the business that targets caring as an objective for its supervisors will indeed be on the right track—possibly even alone among its competitors.

To conclude the point, to focus on caring is not just something that *might* be done by American business executives; it *must* be done in order to develop the kind of competitive productivity demanded by a modern society.

Proactive Focus on Caring

Although we will be dealing specifically with the skill of motivation in Part Four, the following examples of a proactive focus upon caring seem worthy of mention here:

1. *Periodic reminders of importance.* A proactive CEO of a medium-size manufacturer personally conducts monthly meetings of fifty-five supervisors to update them on the company's progress and, literally, to pound home the crucial importance of each supervisor conveying a genuine feeling among his or her staff of each employee's contribution to overall company performance—and to do so on a regular basis.

2. *Periodic evaluations of performance.* It is now formal policy in a large proactive midwestern insurance company that, not less frequently than annually (and occasionally more often), each employee be informed by the immediate supervisor how he or she is doing,

with both words of praise and suggestions for becoming still more productive.

3. *House organ articles.* It is now fairly common practice in proactive companies for employee and other publications to feature success stories of people who moved up in their departments and achieved insider status in the organization.

4. *Luncheon at the top.* A proactive veteran oil and gas executive conducts a monthly competition among all personnel for the best suggestion on how to enhance earning power and/or expense control. First, second, and third prizes are offered, plus a bonus luncheon with the boss for the winner.

5. *Annual career development challenge.* Another proactive president of a large regional bank tosses out an annual goal-setting challenge to all personnel at a 7:00 A.M. breakfast in late December, in the form of a single sheet of paper with one request at the top—"Within ten days, please return this form to your supervisor setting forth your personal (or group) goal (or goals) for the new year."—followed by fifteen blank lines and an invitation at the bottom to accept a twenty-dollar bill at the door when the session is adjourned, with the understanding that either the form or the twenty shall be turned in to department heads with ten days.

What comes through in each of these personal efforts is that, number one, the leader of the business really is personally reaching out to the employees and, number two, somebody really does care at the top. Even so, there's no magic in these five or a hundred other such efforts to enhance morale.

The Downside

At this point it may be in order to give a word of caution to the overly enthusiastic proactive executive. A story from bestselling author Tom Peters illustrates the point nicely. He tells of a highly rewarding telephone call he once received from a former participant in one of his motivational seminars:

"Say, Tom, I thought it would make your day to know that, for about six months now, I have been implementing your morale-building advice to 'catch my people doing it right and commend them for it.' . . . I was just wondering if you might come by the next time you're in these parts and let me show you the difference this has made in our organization; and maybe you can use the experience in a subsequent lecture sometime."

Needless to say, Peters was gratified by such a strong testimonial, and a few weeks later he did go by the plant. He was cheerfully greeted by name and immediately ushered to the CEO's office for coffee and a warm visit. When it was 10:30, the executive indicated to Tom that it was time for him to "catch them winning." For the next full hour, the pair walked through more than a dozen areas, and in each one, the boss found someone to slap on the back or compliment for some mundane reason or other, always with a glad-handed farewell.

Peters was mortified by the spectacle. After the first two or three episodes, he deliberately held back a few paces just to observe the expressions on the faces of the workers. He says that the invariable rolling of the eyes in relief after the boss went by was a sad sight to behold.

Countering Dwindling Morale

It is of course well known that employees with dwindling morale rarely do their jobs well—if they do them at all.

In the introduction to his book *Why Employees Don't Do What They're Supposed to Do and What to Do About It*, Ferdinand F. Fournies describes the plight of managers searching for practical solutions to problems of motivating bad performers:

> As you know, most people at work do most of what they are supposed to do most of the time. They are cooperative, hard-working, and dependable. Some employees do even more than they are supposed to do: they arrive early and stay late; they are nice to have around. But there are those few bad performers who don't seem to do anything right. Unfortunately, there are also those occasions when even the good performers do it wrong or not at all. Have you ever asked yourself, "Why don't they do what they are supposed to do?" Don't feel bad if you didn't get a good answer; most managers are unable to answer that question.
>
> A similar, but larger, question, "Why does man do what he does?" has been the burning question for philosophers, poets, and scientists down through the ages. Psychologists have offered many theories as possible answers

to that question, but in some instances, their answers are not answers at all. For example, you have probably heard that man does what he does because he is motivated to do it; the motivation is the reason. Unfortunately, psychologists don't agree with each other on what motivation is, or how it operates. Some psychologists believe that motivation must always come from within the person, while other psychologists believe that motivation must come from outside the person. Both appear to present equally convincing evidence for their side of this ongoing argument.

Unfortunately, the nuances of this debate are useless to the manager who is trying to get people to produce a quality product or perform a quality service within the constraints of time, cost, and safety. The literature on motivation is confusing to managers searching for a practical answer to the question, "How do *I* motivate *my* people?"

In pursuit of this line of thought, author Fournies continues with a review of the results of his research by identifying what he refers to as his:

Sixteen Hidden Reasons for Employee Nonperformance

1. *They don't know why they should do it.* They don't seem to care because they don't know why they should.
2. *They don't know how to do it.* Telling is not teaching; assuming they know costs you money.
3. *They don't know what they are supposed to do.* Strange but true, we pay them to do a lot of guessing.
4. *They think your way will not work.* Getting people to change is a big problem.
5. *They think their way is better.* Smart people sometimes think the wrong things.
6. *They think something else is more important.* Working on the wrong things is expensive.
7. *There is no positive consequence to them for doing it.* People are moved by rewards, but managers don't use them enough.
8. *They think they are doing it.* After they've done it wrong, it is too late to tell them.
9. *They are rewarded for not doing it.* Managers do it and don't know it.
10. *They are punished for doing what they are supposed to do.* Managers don't mean to do it, but they do.

11. *They anticipate a negative consequence for doing it.* The problem is fear.
12. *There is no negative consequence to them for poor performance.* Managers don't take corrective actions.
13. *Obstacles beyond their control.* Ignoring obstacles will not make them go away.
14. *Their personal limits prevent them from performing.* Managers are confused about people's limitations.
15. *Personal problems.* There is a difference between personal problems and manager's problems.
16. *No one could do it.* Managers misunderstand the problem.

When Motivation Requires Intervention

Professor Fournies goes on to suggest that certain preventive management approaches may bring about better results. He contends that ". . . managers must do specific things at specific times to influence the eventual outcome of their people's performance . . . some occur before the work begins and some occur only after the work begins."

The inhibiting problems *before* work begins are his reasons for nonperformance numbered 1–6, 11, and 13–16. The inhibiting problems *after* work begins are 6–10, 12, 13, and 15. (Thus, numbers 6, 13, and 15 fall into both categories.)

Professor Fournier offers an intervention for each one of these problems, as follows:

Interventions

1. *Before:* Let them know why they should do it.
2. *Before:* Find out if they know how to do it.
3. *Before:* Let them know what they are supposed to do.
4. *Before:* Convince them that your way will work.
5. *Before:* If their way is not better, explain convincingly why it is not better.
6. *Before and After:* Let them know the work priorities.
7. *After:* Verbally reward good performance specifically and frequently.
8. *After:* Give them performance feedback specifically and frequently.
9. *After:* Remove positive consequences for poor performance.

10. *After:* Remove negative consequences for good performance or balance with positive reinforcement.
11. *Before:* Convince them that anticipated future negative consequences for attempting to perform will not occur.
12. *After:* Use negative consequences only with consistent poor performance (progressive discipline).
13. *Before and After:* Verify that there are no obstacles beyond their control.
14. *Before:* Verify that the work is not beyond their personal limits.
15. *Before and After:* Work around personal problems or give the work to someone else.
16. *Before:* Verify that it can be done.

We would be remiss simply to list these additional duties for the boss and leave it at that. It should be pointed out that an innovative boss would not devote a great deal of time to each point but would group them together by means of a well-tailored dialogue. In addition, a well-organized boss would enlist high-level assistance from senior staff members and middle-management supervisors through regular meetings at the operating level. If all of this still seems too complicated or unnecessary, please consider the following truism:

Failure to motivate when intervention is indicated can only sow seeds of mediocre performance at best down the road.

Under the heading of "Friendly Things That Are Easy Enough to Do," Professor Fournies points out eleven examples of common and ordinary courtesies that are regularly violated by well-meaning top-down motivators. While these courtesies are so basic that it's difficult to conceive of anyone at the top of an organization neglecting any of them, we dare not omit them:

- Saying please and thank you
- Looking at people's faces when they are talking to you, and showing a pleasant face
- Greeting people with a good morning or a good afternoon before talking about their work
- Being prompt in keeping appointments so people don't have to waste time waiting for you
- Treating people who come into your office as guests by not making them wait or talk to the top of your head while you

finish your paperwork—or asking them if they will permit you to take a minute or two to complete your paperwork
- Apologizing when you are late or have to interrupt a meeting
- Not insulting people and wasting their time by accepting non-related phone calls during meetings
- Holding conversations with people rather than lecturing them, and not interrupting people when they are speaking
- Controlling your emotional outbursts: You don't have the right to speak loudly or otherwise abuse your employees
- Not making sarcastic comments
- Not eating or drinking while meeting with your employees unless you offer them the same privilege

Unfortunately, there are some managers who aren't friendly at work because they are just not pleasant people in the first place—they aren't friendly to their neighbors or even to their families. Some have even admitted it freely: "I just don't know what comes over me at work. . . . I guess I get so busy there doesn't seem to be time for friendliness." It should of course be just the opposite; that something that comes over you at work should be friendliness.

Perhaps all of this explains what Robert Frost said: "The brain is a wonderful organ. It starts working the moment you awaken and does not stop until you get into the office."

As important as friendliness is, please do not be misled that it will correct or compensate for weak motivation.

The Real Culprit—No "G" Word

Strong motivation begins with the "G" word—"G" is for *goal*. In all "before work begins" and "after work begins" inhibitors cited by Professor Fournies, we believe that the core problem is often the absence of clearly defined objectives.

In Part Six, we suggest that, more than merely reaching our goals, life should be a matter of reaching toward one's full potential. So be it. Yet, it is axiomatic that reaching anyone's full potential is but an amalgam of their intermediate goals. It won't happen without predetermined "G" words along the way.

The real problem with employees who "don't know why they should do it" or "think something else is more important" may simply be that they just don't understand the objectives of their job. Perhaps they're not clearly defined, too complicated, too general, or maybe even nonexistent.

In an effort to pull together the relevant academic notions concerning the impact of motivation upon productivity—i.e., why do people work? Professor Victor H. Vroom of Carnegie Institute of Technology wrote a widely acclaimed book, *Work and Motivation*, published in 1964. He introduced his subject as follows:

> Working by both men and women is so commonplace that the question why people work is seldom asked. We are much more likely to wonder why people climb mountains, drive sports cars or commit suicide than to question the motivational basis of the decision to work. If asked directly why they work, most individuals would probably give a simple answer. They work because there is work to be done, because they like work, or because they need to earn a living. Although these answers contain grains of truth, their apparent simplicity obscures what is, on close examination, an extremely complex and basic problem.

Professor Vroom concluded that there are two types of conditions that affect the likelihood that people will work—economic and motivational. He reasoned that the economic side was driven by a societal demand for goods and services; on the motivational side, he claimed that "given the opportunity, a person will choose to work when the valence of outcomes which he expects to attain from working are more positive than the valence of outcomes which he expects to attain from not working.

It is the motivational aspect of this theorem that is of interest here. Vroom identified five positive determinants of jobs:

1. They provide financial remuneration.
2. They require the expenditure of energy.
3. They involve the production of goods and services.
4. They permit or require social interaction.
5. They affect the social status of the worker.

The implication here is that—in varying degrees, of course—everyone can be motivated by any one, any combination, or even all five of these factors at the same time. In other words, we must *earn* . . . we must *energize* . . . we must *produce* . . . we must *interact* . . . and we seek *status*.

The enlightened managerial leader would do well to tuck these five words away for quick and reliable access later, when motivational strategies are being formulated. In our view, they represent the best ways thus far documented to get the attention of people in the work-place.

A Reliable Launching Pad—The "P" Word

Motivation begins with the "G" word, but it ends with the "P" word, *participation*.

Talking about motivation is a fashionable pastime, but it is but an idle exercise without a launching pad to make it happen effectively. The motivator is powerless until his or her efforts can take off within the group. And we don't believe this can happen very often without the group's participation in selecting the "G" words. It is up to the enlightened managerial leader to decide whether to involve the group to a greater or a lesser degree in the decision making. This generally depends upon the situation—the experience of the group, and the difficulty of the task. Whatever the situation, effective motivators will find a way to bring about the maximum participation—the "P" word—of followers in determining the goals—the "G"word. Effective motivators know that the involvement of those who will be part of the group trying to reach those goals is crucial to the outcome.

Edwin A. Locke and Gary P. Latham's book *Goal Setting—A Motivational Technique That Works!* reported on their exacting research, both in laboratory and field, concerning goal setting. Although they themselves warned that "statistics don't prove causation," their findings seem highly useful, as follows:

- A specific goal and timetable clearly does work better than for people just to be told to "do your best" . . . "as soon as possible."
- Goal setting, in combination with on-site presence of a supervisor, was shown to be the key to improved productivity.
- While different approaches work best under different circumstances, participative goal setting was superior to assigned goal setting, both as to the setting of higher goals and attainment of those goals.

It is the latter one of their conclusions that is most fitting here, as we turn next to what Peter Drucker has to say in *The Practice of Management* about the motivational principle of participative involvement:

This is so important that some of the most effective managers I know go one step further. They have each of their subordinates write a "manager's letter" twice a year. In this letter to his superior, each manager first defines the objectives of his superior's job and of his own job as he sees them. He then sets down the performance standards which he believes are being applied to him. Next, he lists the things he must do himself to attain these goals—and the things within his own unit he considers the major obstacles. He lists the things his superior and the company do that help him and the things that hamper him. Finally, he outlines what he proposes to do during the next year to reach his goals. If his superior accepts this statement, the "manager's letter" becomes the charter under which the manager operates.

Yes . . . efforts to motivate—even those that begin with the "G" word—will probably struggle by comparison with those that also end with the "P" word.

A Quantified Approach

The concept of management has been quantified algebraically by Claude S. George, Jr., Dean of the Graduate School of Management at the University of North Carolina. He found managing to be the sum of our conceptual and physical acts, modified by conceptual and physical environmental factors, and multiplied by a function of all the individual objectives and group objectives involved. Here's the way his formula looks:

$$\text{"}Mg = [\ (Ac + Ap) \rightarrow (Ec + Ep)\ ]\ f\ (Oi,\ Og), \text{ where:}$$
$$Ac\ =\ \text{conceptual acts}$$
$$Ap\ =\ \text{physical acts}$$
$$Ec\ =\ \text{conceptual environment}$$
$$Ep\ =\ \text{physical environment}$$
$$Oi\ =\ \text{individual objectives}$$
$$Og\ =\ \text{group objectives"}$$

Accordingly, we submit that since group performance, by definition, can never amount to more than aggregate individual performance, individual participation in the goal-setting process—both group and individual—is the sine qua non for maximum motivational results. And this motivational launching pad will take its shape and form best through the early participation of the maximum number.

Three More "P" Words—Positive Peer Pressure

At the core of many effective efforts to motivate others is the technique of showing them "how they will benefit" in more positive ways than simply keeping their jobs. In addition to calling the participants' attention to potential benefits, there is another powerful approach known as positive peer pressure—coincidentally, three more "P" words.

Lou Heckler, a prominent motivational consultant, tells a story that illustrates how strong such pressure can be:

"A neighbor of mine had given birth to two boys in less than two years and, shortly afterwards, developed an excess-weight problem. She was talking about it out in the yard one day, and vowed to do something about it." He continued, "I didn't see her for nearly three months and was I surprised! She had really done an incredible job . . . about 25 pounds lighter . . . and was a picture of good health. I soon learned she had enrolled in a national weight reduction organization, and of course I asked about their basic approach. Was it diet? . . . behavioral modification? . . . or what?

"All of that," she replied, "but what really got me was getting weighed in front of all those people. Every other Thursday night, I would step up on the scale and the host would yell '137' to the whole room—and they would write it on this big board opposite my name—and I would literally fall into my own shirt in chagrin. But that's not all . . . he would then ask me how much I intended to lose over the next two weeks . . . and he would write that number up there too . . . and when I came back two weeks later, I'd have to stand up on that scale again."

Positive peer pressure through public goal setting can be amazingly effective. This concept has proven itself over the years in sales organizations where wall charts are used to track both individual and group revenue quotas and attainment. It's the same principle as using the refrigerator at home with those little yellow stickers about who "cleaned their plate," "made their bed," or perhaps "didn't get to class on time." It works well with big kids, too.

Another version of positive peer pressure is what author Tom Peters calls "fabulous brag sessions." He claims there's nothing more fun at a staff meeting than to get up before co-workers and sound off about having done something well. Some may be shy at first, but a little positive reinforcement usually does wonders. The silent ones generally have a two-part reaction: They are happy for the lead-off persons, but a little jealous until they can get up and do the same thing. "Fabulous brag sessions" are one good way to achieve effective motivation through positive peer pressure.

Some organizations have found it productive to hold lots of celebrations. In *Passion for Excellence*, Tom Peters cites the case of a textile factory where the foreman decided to buy some fairly expensive chairs for each worker's station on the assembly line. His technique was ingenious. He decided to announce that all those who exceeded their target output by 25 percent for a month would win a new chair. But it would be awarded in a unique way. The foreman would call the winners to his office, put each one on a new chair, and then roll each winner back to his or her work station! Production improved, and so did the workers' spirits.

The Subtleties of Motivation

Despite all that has been learned about motivation through practical experience and through painstaking research, it must be admitted that there are few if any infallible methods for inspiring others to perform well every time. What worked well under one set of circumstances may fall far short in another.

Even when there are clearly enunciated goals—the "G" word—the results may be inadequate. Perhaps the goals were too ambitious, or not tough enough, or just not at all what the followers would have chosen for themselves. Nor is the "P" word any guarantor of success. Even a group that has participated fully in the goal-setting process may still come up with disappointing results. Perhaps the goals were not precisely quantified, or they may not have been supported by a timetable with intermediate milestones along the way.

Finally, even the most thorough implementation of the principles and techniques of motivation will prove fruitless if a grain of insincerity on the part of the motivator is detectable. Samuel Goldwyn once said: "The most important thing about acting is honesty—once you've learned to fake that, you're in." But in reality, one who would learn to motivate others successfully should never fake anything.

Planning Is Not All There Is

Do not underestimate the value of planning to the role of leadership. Indeed, unplanned leadership would be a misnomer . . . an absolute contradiction in terms. But it is a gross error to go to the other extreme and to overplan.

Organizations and individuals that are totally preoccupied with planning, almost to the exclusion of everything else, are in error. This is a common problem that must be solved. Going beyond planning per se, there are two vital functions that should precede planning and two that should follow.

The Concept of Master Planning

The underlying principle of this section is that master planning—in which planning is only one of five steps—is essential to effective leadership.

In a survey taken of the two hundred largest banking companies in a six-state region, the position of corporate planning in each institution's management process was examined. The following findings came to light:

- All of the respondents (100 percent) confirmed that they engaged in some form of planning.
- All felt that their planning effort was increasingly effective.
- But less than half—44 percent—could state that plans were pre-

ceded and driven by clearly established quantified objectives that were "tough" but believed attainable.
- Only 28 percent could say for sure that such goals were established only after conducting careful research of economic, market, and organizational data.
- About the same proportion—31 percent—stated there was a strong system in place fixing responsibility for the implementation of such plans.
- Only 18 percent had a monthly "scorecard" to monitor variances from plan, in order to make mid-course corrections along the way.
- Just 11 percent were positive that the results from their monitoring system became input for the next year's research for the establishment of new goals.

The inescapable conclusion to be drawn from these figures is that most of these bankers did not really understand the master planning concept. What passed for planning in most banks was merely an annual ritual in which those in charge arbitrarily set all the goals. There seemed to be very little organizational input that was much more than a cursory concern for the marketplace or the economy. Most of these plans were seemingly put on automatic pilot to work for themselves; only rarely could one find a sophisticated scorecard for catching variances, making mid-course corrections, or constructing a better plan for the next year.

The problems revealed by this survey should come as no great shock to those who are familiar with current writings. Here's an example of how one of the best known, Peter F. Drucker, handled it over twenty years ago, in *The Practice of Management*: "Because management is viewed as a process, we best approach the analysis of the process by analyzing the manager's functions of planning, organizing, staffing, directing and controlling." Only our Master Planning Model Step 3 (planning) made the list.

Admittedly, planning itself is the centerpiece of the five-step master planning process, but it's not the "whole enchilada." There are many other pieces necessary to complete the entire picture.

Here are two corollaries from all this for your consideration:

1. Planning can make the difference between an organization on the move and one that drifts.

but

2. Planning cannot be more than a superficial exercise without

research and *goal setting* preceding it and *implementation* and *monitoring* results following it.

A Closer Look

The entire master planning process of five steps is outlined in Figure 7. Following is an explanation of each of those steps.

Step I. Research

- *Economic.* Certainly any plan should be tempered by apparent trends in the economy that could contribute significantly to its success or failure.
- *Market.* Regrettably, too much planning—with or without goal setting—goes on without regard for market considerations (demand, competition, alternative strategies, etc.).
- *Organizational.* Overly ambitious goals and plans may be far beyond the capacity of existing staff to achieve; establishing a realistic timetable to develop such capacity, or formulating more realistic aspirations—or both—could well be a winning strategy.
- *Other.* As needed.

Figure 7.   The five essential steps in our Master Planning Model.

I. Research	II. Goal Setting	III. Planning	IV. Implementation	V. Monitoring Results
Economic	Urgent (now)	Crisis plan	Who?	The scorecard
Market	Short-term (12 months)	Profit plan	What?	Incentive compensation
Organizational	Medium-term (2 to 4 years)	Intermediate plan	When?	Mid-course corrections
Other	Long-term (5 years)	Long-term plan	How (methods, systems, procedures)?	Research for new goals

Step II. Goal Setting

- *Urgent (now)*. Emergency goal setting calls for great poise and insight on the part of the leader.
- *Short-term (twelve months)*. Making an early distinction between short-, medium-, and long-term goals is a necessity for best results; the one-year horizon can hardly be planned without first adopting attainable objectives that will require stretch performance.
- *Medium-term (two to four years)*. Master planners must dare to think beyond the initial twelve months. Above all, goals must be credible and carefully chosen well before the actual planning process begins.
- *Long-term (five years or more)*. With the realization that anything beyond twenty-four months grows more hypothetical with each added year, the real value of setting long-term goals is to provide perspective and balance for intermediate efforts; although attainment of objectives sixty months or beyond will remain in doubt for a long time, the absence of long-term goals can seriously erode a determined outlook and foster inconsistency.

Step III. Planning

- *Crisis plan*. Like urgent goal setting, this will test an organization—especially the leader.
- *Profit plan*. Sometimes called the "business plan," this begins with a focus on the short-term goals previously adopted and on evaluation of what needs to be done by whom and by when. Needless to say, such "whats" must be quantified precisely in order for Step V to be carried out properly.
- *Intermediate plan*. Although this will be replaced by the next year's profit plan, the intermediate plan is geared to medium-term goals beyond one year and provides the best format for setting and assessing objectives for the new year.
- *Long-term plan*. This plan should be assembled with the same basic approach as the other two; that is, the knowledge of who can do what best when (in what length of time). It will be advisable to treat these assignments as if they were expected to be done in a much shorter time frame.

Step IV. Implementation

- *Who?* The leader will want to recall Principles One through Four in making individual and group assignments of planned tasks.

- *What?* The key word here is motivation, in that those assigned will need to buy in on each task that needs to be performed.
- *When?* A timetable can be developed best through a participative dialogue.
- *How?* The methods, systems, and procedures must be at least as sophisticated as the goals and plans themselves; anything less will risk the loss of every other step in the process.

Step V. Monitoring Results

- *The scorecard.* This measurement should be as plain and as clear as possible, so that it will become emblazoned on the memories of all participants, who must also have a clear understanding of the significance of achievements to the organization.
- *Incentive compensation.* The terms of each participant's rewards and benefits should be made completely clear.
- *Mid-course corrections.* A great advantage of monitoring results according to a predetermined plan is that any necessary changes can be made along the way. Such reviews should occur no less than quarterly, and new goals should be formulated with the participation of those who will be doing the work to achieve them.
- *Research for new goals.* At the end of the whole process, the entire body of results monitored becomes the very best data to flow back to Column I, Research, in order to stimulate the MPM all over again (see long right-to-left arrow at the bottom of Figure 7).

More About Organizational Research

As already stated, the leader's intimate knowledge of the strengths and weaknesses of the organization is vital to the outcome of the projects undertaken—especially those projects involving inordinate risk. Our suggested checklist for structuring research so as to determine an organization's strengths and weaknesses would look something like this:

    A. Analysis of human resources
       1. Table of organization
       2. Qualifications
       3. Experience
       4. Training

       5. Structural functions
       6. Structural gaps
       7. Recruiting needs
       8. Other
   B. Analysis of other resources
       1. Liquidity
       2. Fixed assets
       3. Indebtedness
       4. Capital strength
       5. Earning power
       6. Adequacy of equipment
       7. Supplies
       8. Other
   C. Development of a basic organizational philosophy
       1. Corporate mission
       2. Bylaw mandates
       3. Board policies
       4. Commitments to owners
       5. Regulatory constraints
       6. Earnings ambitions
       7. Community obligations
       8. Other

Concerning Part C, the enunciated business philosophy of the Liberty National Bank & Trust Company, Oklahoma City, reads well enough, we think, to share with you:

> **"Maximum sustainable long-range**
> **earning power, consistent with**
> **responsible citizenship**
> **through**
> **superior customer service**
> **designed, monitored, and redesigned**
> **to solve more and more customer problems**
> **more profitably for all."**

Obvious platitudes? . . . Perhaps, but the role of leadership often involves the use of such philosophy to create a vibrant day-to-day culture in which to work and prosper.

An Actual Application of the MPM

When coauthor Bill McLean became President and CEO of Liberty National Bank in 1967, he was confronted by a set of circumstances

that caused him to invoke the Master Planning Model. Here's his
story, in brief:

> From my second day on duty, it became fairly normal for
> me to receive at least two or three questions per day as to
> when we would begin construction on a new drive-in
> banking facility. Either in the corridors, on the elevators,
> or by telephone, the questions kept coming.
>
> Because of congestion and fumes in the ancient drive-
> through facility, a new one was critically needed, and some
> months earlier my predecessor had taken an option on a
> building site to the west of our building, just within the
> 1000-foot maximum distance required by law. It was not in
> a desirable section of the downtown area and would re-
> quire a construction cost of between $800,000 and $1 mil-
> lion. Somehow, the long-term implication of that kind of
> investment in that location was not very appealing.
>
> In any case, my first obligation was to get acquainted
> quickly with my officers and—simultaneously, if possi-
> ble—to gain a rapid and accurate impression of how well
> the bank's overall mission was being fulfilled. So, while
> mulling over the pressing drive-in construction decision, I
> called a meeting of the ninety officers in the boardroom—
> not enough space to have such a meeting, but the only one
> available. There were only enough seats to accommodate a
> twenty-five-person board, so we all stood.
>
> After some brief opening remarks, I distributed a one-
> page questionnaire that read:
>
> 1. What do you consider Liberty's number-one exter-
>   nal need to be?
> 2. What do you consider Liberty's number-one inter-
>   nal need to be?
> 3. What is the number-one need in your area of re-
>   sponsibility?
>
> There was also a signature line with the word optional un-
> derneath it. I asked for a return of the questionnaire within
> ten days. Interestingly, they were all back in half that time,
> and each one was signed.
>
> If we could have collated all the responses to the first
> two questions in a computer—which we didn't do in those
> days—the aggregate results would have looked like this:

1. Liberty's number one external need is to have a stronger public presence.
2. Liberty's number one internal need is to convey a clearer sense of direction.

Our senior executives thought about these provocative findings along with some of our crucial space problems over the weeks that followed, and we ultimately concluded that the crucial need was not a new drive-in nearly so much as an entirely new home with its own new drive-in facility.

In a comparatively short time, with the confirming advice of a prominent real estate consulting firm, the directors authorized the building of Liberty Tower three hundred feet east of the old bank, with its drive-in one block and a half to the north. Obviously, premature construction of an automobile banking facility to the west of the old location would have made such a decision impossible, and that's a little scary. It would have anchored the bank for too many more years in an inferior location.

Early one morning, as I drove downtown, it came to me in a flash. Those who had peppered me with all those questions as to when we would build the drive-in were really operating way out in Column IV (Implementation) of the MPM—they were, in effect, inquiring when we would implement a plan, the goal of which had never been clearly enunciated or based, in the first place, upon any thorough research. For example, the question had never even been asked: "How long should Liberty remain in a building that had never been designed with the prospect of housing the largest financial institution of a four-state region?" And they certainly had not related such a decision to the bank's priority needs—external as well as internal.

Who can say what the skyline of Oklahoma City would look like today had it not been for the Master Planning Model (MPM) and the concept of implementing actions based upon soundly conceived plans and tied to carefully selected goals, which, in turn, were set only after thoroughly conducting appropriate research.

We repeat, with emphasis, that planning itself cannot stand alone: It must be *preceded* by both research and goal setting and *followed* by implementation and monitoring results. As for the latter, within twelve months of the move to Liberty Tower, the bank had completed its jump from fourth position in the state three years earlier to a strong first place!

The point is that, without master planning, you can only expect to flounder in today's world. Beyond this, the act of planning itself is simply not all there is to the process.

A Leader's Sense of Direction: Where Does It Fit?

Harvard Business School Professor of Leadership Dr. Abraham Zaleznik, a clinical psychologist, has earned international renown for his research in the field. In his 1989 book, *The Managerial Mystique*, he wrote that "true leaders, through the exercise of vision, seem to overcome the conflict between order and chaos. . . . They focus on *what* to do rather than *how* to do things. . . . such vision is what projects an organization's destiny."

Countless other academicians, motivational consultants, and leaders in nearly every field talk and write constantly about vision being an essential ingredient, if not the core quality, of a leader. Here are three business leaders among the many whose vision projected the destiny of their companies:

- Tom Monahan, of the small community of Ypsilanti, Michigan (just outside of Ann Arbor), conceived of delivering a good, hot pizza to the customer's front door in less than thirty minutes. The multimillion-dollar result is the nationwide chain, Domino's Pizza.
- Fred Smith, a student at Yale, sensed that the best way to deliver a package overnight from city to city—even from Los Angeles to San Francisco—is through Memphis. The result is an entire industry, with Fred's Federal Express leading the way.
- The story is told of a tourist at fabulous Disney World in Orlando, Florida, remarking, "What a shame Mr. Disney never saw all of this." . . . "Oh, but he did," replied the guide, "that's why it's here!"

How do we square an individual's vision with our Master Planning Model and the participatory process of conducting research and setting goals? If it is the function of leadership to run the show by bringing the best thinking of the group together, what about the leader's vision . . . the sense of direction that probably made him or her the leader in the first place?

The answer is very plain: What the leader feels about the ultimate direction should be the foundation and the motivating force of the research that is conducted in the first stage of the MPM (Column I). When the process moves to Column II, the leader must exert strong, positive influence in setting the goals so that they embody or at least incorporate his or her vision. This is a centripetal process, a coming together of the best that the leader and the group have to offer. Third, as we shall see in Part Four, there's a cardinal rule of leadership: Under certain urgent circumstances, the leader may and in fact occasionally must preempt the whole process. In such instances, of course, the MPM may have to be laid aside temporarily or perhaps even completely abandoned for an extended period. Yes . . . vision and the executive decision are still very much alive.

The main point of this discussion is that the Master Planning Model is a strong and useful template that can fit nicely over almost any group endeavor. But planning by itself is only one of MPM's five distinct, closely interrelated steps. With the leader's sense of direction always in play, the principle of master planning is a highly reliable tool that can be used frequently and quite profitably in most organizations.

Building Relationships Is a Leadership Imperative

"We talk about quality of product and service. But what about the quality of our relationships and the quality of our communications and the quality of our promises to each other?"—Max De Pree, CEO of Herman Miller, Inc.

Leadership is by definition a relationship between leader and follower(s). Leadership has all of the elements that one normally thinks of in any human relationship, including trust, confidence, and true appreciation for the other. Strong, positive interpersonal relationships lead to the belief that each person has the other's best interests at heart, that each wishes to take care of the feelings and those things the other person considers to be important, and that each accepts some responsibility for the other person's well-being. But how are positive relationships developed? What are the dynamics and mechanisms by which all of this takes place? Let us try and unravel relationships in order to learn what they are and what they are not. For if you are to lead, you surely must understand this important aspect of human endeavor.

Properties of Relationships

Relationships may be characterized in the same way that one can describe groups. They have the properties of purpose, interdependence, limits or boundaries, control by their own rules, mutual understanding of group reality, and a tendency toward an expansive view of the group as somehow greater than the sum of the qualities of its individual members.

All relationships have the same properties but in any number of different combinations and forms. A leader first must be a part of the relational situation and second must work within the constraints of that situation's properties to help the group accomplish its tasks. Success as a leader is strongly influenced by the extent to which the person attempting to lead is able to position him- or herself with respect to these properties. See Figure 8 for a checklist of relationship properties that the successful leader consciously or fortuitously works within. Failing to act in a manner consistent with this list will detract from a leader's ability to influence the members of the relationship.

Consider the interactions of the members of a work team. First, they recognize that they are there to work rather than play. They also develop a particular approach to working, with an understanding of what is supposed to happen and what each member of the team is to do in order to reach their goal.

The members of the team know how to approach each other and what the acceptable limits are for their interaction with one another. Over time, they learn that Janice can be teased and George cannot. The workers also recognize who is really "on the team"—that is, who is committed to the group and not on its fringes. Work teams develop a set of expectations about what behavior is acceptable, what level of work is acceptable, who can be counted on under pressure, and many other things about members' actions.

Those within the relationship develop common perceptions of

Figure 8. Properties of relationships and related leader actions.

Properties	Leader Action
Purpose	Recognize group purpose
Interdependence	Understand how members are connected
Limits	Work within relationship boundaries
Control	Operate consistent with expectations
Group reality	Stay within group knowledge limits
Greater than sum	Mobilize members to stretch and grow

how it is to work in their present situation, how to react to others in other parts of the work setting outside of their team, and a whole host of other "facts" that make up group reality. The members of a highly integrated or cohesive team take pride in their ability to accomplish things together that they believe they could not do alone.

Leaders must operate within the boundaries of these six properties if they are to influence the other members of the relationship. Leadership actions have to be consistent with a team's purpose. Advocating a change in purpose, which at times may be necessary, requires a reorientation of the relationship. Successful leaders avoid acting at cross-purposes to the group's purpose or goal(s), unless this is a necessity for the survival of the relationship.

The successful leader recognizes and accepts the various linkages and dependencies among the members. Failing to operate consistently within these interdependencies will slow down or even block a leader's attempts to influence others. It is more efficient to work within the group's existing conditions than to forge new connections between members. Attempting to change existing interpersonal ties means first disrupting them and then making new ones. Sometimes, of course, this action is required to accomplish some task. But when it is not required, the leader usually is better served by staying with what everyone involved understands and is comfortable with.

Smart leaders operate within the boundaries (limits) and according to the rules (control) of the group. They approach an issue about which there is some need for leadership from the perspective of the group (group reality). They integrate all of this into the "big picture," the vision of the solution to the issue affecting those in the relationship. Through leader action, those in the relationship tend to view the relationship as instrumental in achieving goals that an individual could not achieve alone (greater than the sum).

Flexibility and Cohesion: Key Dimensions of Relationships

Relationships are not static, they change and evolve. Members of a relationship are drawn together through an appreciation for one another. They tend to adjust to the pressures placed upon them from outside the relationship as well as to pressures that arise from within the relationship (flexibility). As the members of the relationship take on a feeling of "us," they are more willing to forgo a strict individual orientation and to sacrifice their own goals for the sake of the relationship (cohesion). This begins with the process of negotiation between members about issues over which they disagree. As this "us" feeling evolves, members describe the relationship as increasingly cohesive.

Cohesion begins when members initially come together as disengaged individuals who find themselves attracted to other members for some reason. As this attraction increases, the members feel closer to each other and begin to draw support from one another. As the support increases, members become involved with each other, learning more and more about the others including their personal feelings and sometimes even their aspirations or dreams.

This process seems to unfold in the decision-making process. When group members have only a slight interest in the wishes of the others, there will be little group involvement in decision making. Individuals will make decisions alone and primarily for their own purposes. As the involvement grows through members understanding the benefits of the relationship, however, they develop much more concern about the consequences of the decisions for each other and for the group.

At the point where members are highly supportive of the others, where there is much between-member consultation before decisions are made, and where members feel a loyalty to each other, the relationship is described as "enmeshed." The relationship is highly cohesive, and members share interests and activities, a feeling of unity, and pride in the relationship. There is a high level of commitment to the other members.

Obviously, the extremes of this dimension of cohesion have to be avoided. Relationships that have too little cohesion will lack sufficient common interest for collective action and are likely to break apart. At the other extreme is the relationship that is so highly intertwined that there is a blurring of individuality. Only the group good is considered, and the wishes of the individual are not addressed.

Once a relationship has existed for some time, expectations develop. Norms emerge for the way members relate to each other. As those in the relationship gain experience with each other, they learn about what they have in common with the others, including a common set of values. This discovery process continues, stabilizing the relationship. Developing cohesion generally starts with little common interest at the initial stage—a somewhat unpredictable situation—and eventually moves to the point where everything seems to be prescribed and ritualized and where member interactions become very rigid. This continuum reflects the degree of flexibility within the relationship.

Phases in Relationships

Relationships pass through phases. In their book *Connecting with Self and Others*, Miller, Wackman, Nunnally, and Miller discuss the four phases that members of a relationship tend to experience. These phases are not necessarily linear, with one leading to another in a predictable way. Sometimes the relationship moves back and forth between two phases. Occasionally, the group tends to stay in one particular phase for a long period. Some members of the relationship who get "stuck" in one phase eventually end their participation in that relationship without moving to other phases.

These four phases are found in all kinds of relationships—business, social, personal. They also tend to occur in a progression in the following sequence:

1. Visionary
2. Adversarial
3. Dormant
4. Vital

As a leader, you need to be aware of these phases so that you may understand where those in the relationship stand with each other and with you. Then you can utilize your communications skills to enhance the positive and reduce the negative impact within each phase.

Visionary Phase

This phase begins with an imaginary view of the future in the relationship. This view is generally positive, with expectations for favorable outcomes for oneself from the relationship. In fact, there is a tendency to emphasize the positive and overlook or minimize the negative at this stage. Energy levels and excitement tend to be high as the members focus on themselves and on each other's immediate future. This phase can occur at times other than the beginning of a relationship. It may occur within a relationship that is in need of renewal.

Members set directions for themselves and for the relationship. They use the excitement and enthusiasm to get the relationship off to a good start. Motivation is high as members reinforce one another's views of the future. They are optimistic at this stage, believing that they can accomplish their vision of reality. Unfortunately, this shared vision may also be a distorted picture of what the future holds. Optimism causes members to overlook or discount the downside risks in the situation. Focusing on the opportunities within the relationship can lead to unrealistic expectations of what others in the relationship can deliver. Members may tend to deny what does not fit with their vision of success. They may even overlook indications or behaviors from others that might interfere with the successful accomplishment of their vision. Members want to see the others as relating positively to their dream coming true.

By the same token, the desire to be seen by the others as they want to be seen may lead members to behave deceptively in order to meet what they believe others wish them to be. Or, members' high expectations for themselves may lead them to behave deceptively or inconsistently with the way they would normally behave. Members tend to do this rather than disrupt the hope for a successful future.

The visionary phase is an important one because it is not possible for leadership to occur without the leader projecting a sense of future success to the members of the relationship. The first leader action is establishing with the followers a picture of future success. But, as we have observed, leaders need to be mindful of both the positive and the negative side of creating the vision of the future.

Adversarial Phase

At some point, unfortunately, reality tends to intrude upon the group's rosy vision of the future. Members may have difficulty sustaining their optimism as complex issues arise and frustration sets in. They become disappointed and may even be disillusioned. To protect themselves, members project the cause of their disappointment onto other members. In this phase, each member initially fails to see his or her own shortcomings.

Instead of denying what is undesirable about others, as was done in the visionary phase, members now focus on the problems, often seeing them as worse than they really are. Differences are highlighted, while points of agreement or similarities tend to be discounted. Each member wants the others to change rather than accepting that he or she may have to change, too.

The positive side of this phase is that reality is introduced into the relationship and members tend to own up to who they are. As members are forced to recognize each other's true needs and wishes, they begin to develop a more honest, less distorted view of their associates. This tends to strengthen the relationship. Working through conflicts generally leads to an acceptance of the other members. But without the leader's using effective communication skills to work through these differences, the relationship may reach an impasse and then dissolve.

A lot of negative activity can occur in the adversarial phase. Members may attempt to remake one another into what they are not. Or they may turn their disappointments inward on themselves. Or all of this negative feeling can lead to disruptions between members. These disruptions often predispose the members to consider other relationships with the new visionary hope of a brighter future there.

Leadership in the adversarial phase involves absorbing some of the disappointment brought on by the unfulfilled expectations members feel from one another. The leader needs to redirect the members' angry feelings and frustrations into a more realistic acceptance of each other. Only then can those in the relationship constructively approach the issues and opportunities facing the group.

It is through such leadership initiatives that those in the adversarial phase can avoid a breakup of the relationship. If the relationship does not end or move out of this phase, the members may become embittered and cynical. Often they stay within the relationship because of other reasons, such as religious convictions or for the sake of the children (in marriage), or because they desire to continue to meet their financial obligations or to retain benefits and, ultimately, retirement (in work relationships). Fortunately, movement from this phase to a new phase in the relationship is a likely outcome.

Dormant Phase

This phase is characterized by acceptance within the relationship. Realism is the basis for the members' perceptions of themselves, of their situation, and of the issues they face. The members gain perspective from their experience within the relationship, enabling them to handle potentially disruptive events with equanimity. There is at least an outward calm even if there is some inward discontent. Differences are tolerated, and the others in the relationship are taken for granted. Members may not feel the need to spend time with the others in the relationship, believing that they know their points of view.

Depending upon the level of cohesion among the members, this period can be marked by feelings of peace or of emptiness. Often both feelings are present, for few relationships completely meet all of their members' needs. In sum, members seem content to focus on meeting their own needs and developing their individuality within the apparently secure relationship. They take greater responsibility for what is happening to them, thus do not need to project their shortcomings onto others. Less energy is needed to operate in the dormant phase.

This phase can provide needed rest between the more intense phases, thus allowing members to renew their energies.

With the major focus upon themselves, members may become overly concerned about what they as individuals want and spend too little time on what others in the relationship want. Issues may resolve themselves without being directly addressed by group members. The cohesion of the group often declines as members learn to operate on their own. Without some precipitating event to bring it alive again, the dormant phase continues until the relationship dissolves.

Leadership during the dormant phase takes into account the individuality of the members of the relationship. This includes listening to their ideas, needs, aspirations, and wishes. The leader is then able to link his or her vision and goals with those of the other members so that they all can realistically expect a successful return on their actions.

The danger of the dormant phase is that it can lead the relationship into deterioration. As a leader, you must recognize the need to provide some reason to move out of dormancy and into vitality, the next phase of relationship. In order to do this, you may be able to identify some important opportunity or to help the group recognize some impending crisis.

Leadership can also occur in response to some issue or shock to the relationship that requires everyone to refocus attention on a collective response to this disruption of dormancy. You can help the members do this by reframing the disruption to show how it threatens the relationship and how important the relationship is to everyone involved in it. Your actions can help members realize that being a part of the relationship is as important as meeting their own personal needs.

Vital Phase

A failure to respond successfully to some challenge or opportunity for the relationship generally leads to dissolution of the relationship. The challenge may be stressful or it may be some opportunity, perhaps one that will benefit only some of the relationship members. However, even a partial opportunity has implications for the others as well. It is at this point that a good leader helps members make informed choices among alternatives. You can do this by leading the members to define realistically what is happening to the relationship and to each of them.

The alternative selected may bring the members to a conscious decision to pursue the challenge collectively within the relationship, or they may decide to separate and address it as one or more subunits. If the commitment to the relationship is strong (high cohesion), it is based upon a realistic self-appraisal by each member or on a realistic evaluation of the other(s) and of their mutual interdependence. If the relationship has a long history, is stable, and is based on a recognition that those involved are better off together than separated, then a successful leader should be able to help those in the relationship find a way to address the challenge together.

During the vital phase, members spend time learning who the other(s) are now. Interaction improves; there is interest and energy and greater intensity. Not that everything is necessarily harmonious. Conflicts may be intense, but they are dealt with directly rather than being hidden and smoothed over. Resolution of the issues does not involve questioning the relationship; it does involve searching for appropriate solutions.

Leadership during the vital phase is exhilarating. You can spend more time working on the issues confronting the relationship than on the interpersonal entanglements that often seem to sap so much time and energy. The commitment to others in the relationship is there, as members grow and develop in positive ways.

From Joy Through Discipline: Leaders' Reactions to Issues

The nature of the issue(s) facing those in the relationship has a strong influence over how leaders and members respond to each other, to the demands from the issue(s), and to attempts to provide leadership with respect to the issue(s). Therefore, it is important that leaders understand how issue characteristics can influence their actions and ultimately their effectiveness.

There are three major characteristics of issues that influence relationships and that usually require some conscious response from those in the relationship. Of course, it is possible to identify more than three characteristics. However, these three are useful to illustrate not only how the issues influence leader action but also how these issues must be viewed and dealt with through leader action.

1. *Importance.* Some issues are perceived as being crucial for the success of the relationship or for its members; other issues may be important but are perceived as being part of the pe-

riphery or background for the members or for the relationship.

2. *Pleasantness.* Some issues are very pleasing to those who address them, while some at the other end of the scale are highly distasteful.

3. *Novelty.* Some issues are highly unique, interesting, or challenging to those who address them; others are relatively routine or even mundane, with little inherent satisfaction involved in doing them.

Although these characteristics are more accurately understood as continua, in Figure 9 they are represented as bipolar characteristics in order to reduce the complexity of considering how they can combine and influence group members' responses to a task.

As discussed earlier, leadership occurs in response to some issue or challenge. But the nature of that response will depend on how important or how pleasant or how novel the challenge is. Leaders thus must learn how to vary their approaches, and these three characteristics can be a kind of checklist for you to use to help guide your responses.

In addition, you can use these characteristics to help you understand how the relationship is operating. If most of the issues being addressed in the relationship are perceived to be routine, unpleasant, and unimportant it may be difficult to keep the members interested in remaining in that relationship unless the relationship is highly cohesive or unless the members feel there is great personal value for staying.

Figure 9. Characteristics of issue(s) that face(s) those in relationships.

Characteristic	Characteristics as Combinations of Their Polarities							
Importance	Hi	Hi	Hi	Hi	Lo	Lo	Lo	Lo
Pleasantness	Pls	Pls	Upls	Upls	Pls	Pls	Upls	Upls
Novelty	Unqe	Rout	Unqe	Rout	Unqe	Rout	Unqe	Rout

Key:

Hi = High	Pls = Pleasing	Unqe = Unique
Lo = Low	Upls = Unpleasant	Rout = Routine

Discipline is obviously one important personal characteristic leaders rely on to help them successfully carry out their tasks. You can use the three task characteristics in Figure 9 as a kind of template or overlay to review and to categorize all of the issues and tasks to which you put a hand.

To Do or Not to Do

George Will, the columnist and TV commentator, has observed that one of the decisions every candidate for elected office should make is whether they want most to "be something" or to "do something." Of course, some politicians would admit to wanting both very much. And, indeed, many who desire just to "be something" will, over time, try hard to "do something" in order to get there.

Mr. Will's observation is applicable beyond the world of elections and public office. In building strong relationships with others, enlightened leaders in whatever field understand this principle very well and know, too, the value of making an early and accurate assessment of the category in which each person falls. Some most want to be the star players, but others believe that belonging to a winning team is more important.

One manifestation of this basic psychological struggle has been apparent among certain television performers. Quite often, one of the costars of a popular series will suddenly leave the show and look for other opportunities. Rather than continue as mere participants in a successful program run, these performers seem literally driven to "be someone" independent of the group. Many then come to realize that being a member of a winning team wasn't really so bad, and—guess what—they knock down doors to return.

This same conflict may well be going on in those with whom you would build relationships. Thus, the ability to sense clearly which of the two categories you are dealing with can be a highly useful key to the strength and durability of the relationship you will be able to build.

Sage Advice

Building relationships can be both highly rewarding and devastatingly traumatic. The latter is perhaps the kind of thinking that spawned Henny Youngman's cynical one-liner: "If you need a real friend, buy a dog."

Moreover, building relationships seems to be a never-ending process. The old story of the elderly couple seated before the fire on the eve of their fiftieth wedding anniversary illustrates the point. "I'm mighty proud of you," said he. "What did you say?" she asked. In a much louder voice, he declared, "I SAID . . . I'M MIGHTY PROUD . . . OF YOU!" "Yes", she boomed right back, "AND I'M SICK AND TIRED OF YOU TOO!"

Summary: The Metallic Thread

As we suggested earlier, the building of relationships runs like a metallic thread through each of the principles explained in this section of the book, culminating in Principle 6, "Building Relationships Is a Leadership Imperative."

In the beginning, Principle 1, we observed how leadership must begin with greater self-knowledge because knowing more about ourselves is indispensable to our relationship-building efforts.

In Principle 2, we found that leadership, almost by definition, involves building strong personal relationships with others, not just managing them.

In Principle 3, we saw that the leadership mantle is earned through achievement, usually involving relationships.

Principle 4 states that effective motivational efforts, using the "G" word and the "P" word, will fall short without early emphasis upon careful relationship building.

And, in Principle 5, we found that any attempt to apply the Master Planning Model in a group would have to be preceded by the building of good relationships with the followers.

Thus, without the metallic thread of Principle 6 on relationship building, none of the first five principles can be expected to serve very well.

PART FOUR

The Six Leadership Skills

(What Leaders Need to Be Able to Do)

The time finally comes when one must rise above principle—and learn a skill.

—Anonymous

In leadership—as in most other human pursuits—comprehension of
underlying *principles* alone, without mastery of related *skills* and how
best to *apply* them, affords little assurance of success. Having proposed a thorough appreciation of the half dozen leadership principles
put forth in Part Three, therefore, we present here the six key skills
that we feel would-be leaders must also address:

1. Communications (toward better understanding)
2. The ability to recognize which of three practical roles to play
   as leader
3. Motivation through "inward marketing"
4. Risk management and handling fears
5. Problem solving (including decision making)
6. Relationship renewal (an essential leadership skill)

But before we proceed with our presentation and analysis of these six basic leadership skills, we again offer some caveats.

FIRST, there are of course other skills which may well come into play in any given leader/follower situation; our chosen six are by no means preclusive—rather they are, to us, invaluable in most cases, irrespective of the dynamics involved.

SECOND, mastery of these basic skills alone cannot ensure success.

THIRD, the understanding of our six fundamental leadership principles is another essential ingredient.

FOURTH, there is a literal chasm between merely understanding leadership skills and knowing how to *apply* them for long-term success (the subject of Part Five).

Situational Discretion

(Recognizing Which of Three Roles to Play)

When it comes right down to "doing" leadership, there is no better place to begin than to focus upon the basic alternatives available to a leader for making decisions. We are referring here to decisions that involve others, who in turn will both implement the decisions and be affected by their consequences.

The Three Conventional Choices

Let's bring it all down to 8:00 A.M. next Monday morning as you walk into your office. You're the relatively new chief executive of a medium-size business . . . offering both products and services . . . beset with tough competition and occasional labor unrest . . . having had recent turnover on the senior staff but with experienced middle managers . . . rooted in a solid customer base . . . with a low debt-to-worth ratio . . . and having a record of acceptable earnings. In short, things are generally going OK, but it is clearly not a business that will run itself, at least not very well for very long, and you are the new boss—only four months in office.

Right before your eyes, desk center, are three problems demanding your full attention and prompt disposition. Let's call them problems X, Y, and Z.

PROBLEM X

Turnover at the senior staff level has freed up three parking spaces in the executive garage. Your administrative executive vice-president has provided you with a list of twelve candidates who would really appreciate this perquisite, both symbolically and in terms of the tremendous convenience during inclement weather. Your EVP has offered to relieve you of the decision, either on his own authority or by assembling an ad hoc committee of senior officers to meet and decide on three names for your final approval. *How do you proceed?*

PROBLEM Y

One of the company's top financial consultants has addressed to you a confidential report proposing a fairly large merger with one of your suppliers, a company that has a good management and a strong record of profitability. You realize that the report represents several months of careful analysis. The consolidation, through integration, would widen your margin of profit significantly, but you would have to go through the usual challenge of molding the two executive staffs amicably. The company's debt-to-worth ratio would move somewhat higher, but if earnings developed as predicted, the debt level would be back down to current levels in just thirty months. Your inclination is to try and work it out. *How do you proceed?*

PROBLEM Z

Although the company's earning power has been enviable in recent years, the independent auditors have called to your attention a disturbing escalation in General and Administrative Expense category for six consecutive years. In the same period, the compound rate of growth was 18 percent, and the last two years were up 24 percent and 29 percent, respectively. You have concluded, with help from the independent auditors, that a cut in administrative expenses of at least 12 percent would be highly desirable for next year, with much tighter controls put in place in subsequent years. A decision needs to be made before the end of the month as to how best go about it. *How do you proceed?*

There they are: not uniformly exciting to be sure, but each demanding a decision by you—and right away.

The expression "right away" may well provide a bit of slack at times, but, let's face it, these three problems really won't change very much over time. In fact, your undue delay in making a decision will only:

- *For X,* generate negative morale
- *For Y,* risk losing a rare opportunity for enhancing future earning power
- *For Z,* send the wrong message throughout the organization that expense control is unimportant

So, in the real world, we simply don't always enjoy what we shall call analytical luxury, the time to sit back and slowly evaluate all the possible approaches. What the real world often demands is that the leader's mind be made up without delay. What it comes down to is a very simple and practical choice among three conventional alternatives:

1. Declaring what the decision shall be—*telling*
2. Persuading those involved what the decision should be—*selling*
3. Democratically letting the decision be congealed in the group—*jelling*

For all practical purposes, then, whatever intellectual twist you may try to give it, as a leader you've got only three practical choices.

The Leader's Predicament

In Figure 10, the responsibility (vertical axis) for the results varies directly with the degree to which the authority (horizontal axis) is shared between the leader and the group. When the leader *tells* what the decision shall be, the group exerts no authority and therefore bears none of the responsibility; when the leader *sells* the group on the correct decision, the authority and the responsibility are shared about equally between leader and group; and when the leader lets the decision *jell* democratically within the group, the authority and the responsibility of the group approach 100 percent.

Clearly, your choice depends very much upon the circumstances involved. The leadership skill here is to recognize which of the three choices is most appropriate. Anyone of the following circumstances would seem to justify selecting the telling option:

Figure 10.   The decision diagonal.

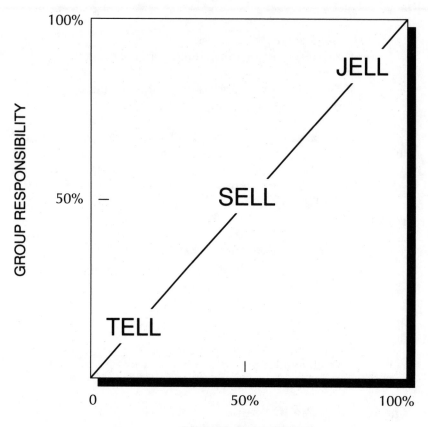

- When there is limited time
- When the pertinent facts are too complex
- When the matter is too confidential
- When the leader simply cannot risk the outcome of a group decision
- When the leader alone feels best qualified to make the decision

Whatever choice is made, there is a powerful overriding truth that deserves mention. In each instance, the leader should try to move up as high as possible on the decision diagonal illustrated in the figure. The reason for this is contained in these simple lines:

Tell me—I'll forget . . .
Show me—I may remember . . .
Involve me—I'll involve others . . .

More and more, as we consider the leader's predicament of choice, the more convinced we are that, over the long term, a leader's effectiveness is determined by his or her growing capacity to know how and when to move confidently up or down the decision diagonal. Not that this movement should be too frequent. Once you have chosen one of the three, you should pretty much try to stay with that choice even if the going gets a bit rough.

Your Two-Minute Warning

It's now time to reach a decision on your choices for problems X, Y, and Z. Let's say that you have two minutes on the clock before declaring whether you want to tell, sell, or jell on each of these three. Which shall it be, and more importantly, WHY?

While you're agonizing on what to do, we will admit that the tell/sell/jell setup is not altogether original. There are other so-called non-contingency approaches, too, including:

- The three classic styles (proposed by the team of Douglas McGregor, Lyndall Urwick, and William Ouchi): X, authoritarian; Y, participative; and Z, consensus
- The Peter Block labels: expert/pair of hands/and consensus
- The Mark Frohman labels: give/give and take/and participative management (PM)
- The Jan P. Muczyk and Bernard C. Reimann labels: directive autocrat/directive democrat or permissive autocrat/and permissive democrat

Whatever alternative terminologies are preferred, the real leadership challenge is posed by the many situations that simply will not accommodate extensive participation time. When these circumstances occur, leaders themselves must act as resources to their followers, either by preempting the decision-making role or daring to risk the involvement of others—if only by trial and error.

In serving as resources for their followers, leaders are therefore involuntarily charged with an essential and inescapable obligation. It is so basic to leadership that Warren Bennis, a widely recognized authority on the subject, has called it the crucial X-factor: the obligation to educate followers.

Answers!

That's it . . . the pistol shot ending the game . . . your time has expired . . . and here are our solutions:

PROBLEM X

There are two courses of action to avoid here. First, do not turn this one over to a committee. Obviously, each executive would lobby strongly for his or her own favorite . . . and those who lose will not soon forget your ignoring their judgment. Second, do not let your EVP take over and play politics with this one.

On the positive side, what better chance for you, the new boss, to get acquainted quickly with your best middle managers. Take the time that you would spend discussing the matter with the committee or the EVP and familiarize yourself with the performance records of the top twelve candidates for the three vacant parking spaces. Then you might do some subtle checking (verbally) with your top executives to confirm your inclinations. When you've made the decision, call in your three winners for a personal visit. This is an occasion you can use to begin a strong new personal bonding that will be pure gold to you over time, as you adjust to your new duties.

PROBLEM Y

One of the givens stated about this situation is that you—the CEO—were inclined to "work it out" and go ahead with the merger. This being the case, letting the decision congeal democratically in the group (i.e., jell) is clearly not the preferred solution. . . . Why gamble on a negative outcome?

By the flipside of the same token, declaring what the decision shall be (i.e., tell) is hardly a wise choice either, because no one else will then feel any responsibility for making a success of the "boss's merger."

So, go in there and sell it, Boss! Be the leader who catapults the company years ahead through this timely consolidation. Explain your rationale, communicate your enthusiasm, and win the group to your way of thinking. Then you will have them working with you in making the merger a success, because they too will feel partially responsible.

PROBLEM Z

Obviously, as the boss, you have every right to decree an across-the-board cut of 12 percent (i.e., tell) and let it go at that. Some executives prefer this approach to expense control over all others. It leaves no chance for confusion because the edict comes from the top. And there is little question as to group performance because everyone must either follow the budget or suffer the consequences.

In this situation, however, you as the new CEO are probably the least informed of the top executives concerning the expense budget. As stated, for the past six years, the company has failed to stay within the budget, and the variances have gotten progressively worse.

This looks like a perfect case for the jell solution. Let your top executives deliberate on just how best to reduce last year's General and Administrative Expense by 12 percent. Who better to put a bright light on those items that need cutting most than the people who have been involved with the overspending in the past?

Have You Noticed?

Our three alternatives, tell, sell, and jell correspond to the three classic styles of leadership—X, Y, and Z. And it is no coincidence that the model problems were labeled X, Y, and Z, corresponding to the styles we recommend for their solution. This was by design not only for ease of memory but also for ease of identification of similar situations.

As you become more skillful in your various leadership roles, remember the desirability of moving up the decision diagonal with more and more discretionary decisions. Let's call it *managing up*.

SKILL 2

Communications

(Toward Fostering a Better Understanding)

Your success in putting into practical use the principles and techniques of leadership as described in this book will be directly dependent upon your ability to communicate. Indeed, communication has long been recognized as the essential organizational skill.

The Key Elements of Communication

Accordingly, as we discuss this leadership skill we acknowledge the enormity of the subject and state at the outset that we shall not here give detailed instructions on how to make a speech or write a memo. We shall instead concentrate on the key elements of communication that serve to foster better understanding between leaders and followers.

Perceptivity

Since the 1960s, authoritarian leadership has been out of favor in most organizations. Whereas so-called teams and families of workers formerly could be *told* what to do, now *consent* and *coalition* have become the watchwords for organizational success.

Does this mean that style X, the tell approach, is dead? . . . Not at all, though it has become obsolete in many circumstances. Bosses still set salaries (sometimes being required to get the directors' approval) and tell who has responsibility for getting a particular job done—and undoubtedly a great deal more in some organizations. But the enlightened head of an organization rules through the consent of the governed most of the time. The leader becomes a student of the organization and, as such, learns to cope with followers' indifference to his or her personal identity. This has been referred to as "frailty in others." "The boss" should "expect it" for best results. Above all, do not let such indifference feed any latent insecurities needing to be nourished. Once that happens, leadership is gone.

If you want to become a more perceptive communicator, you must develop good insight and knowledge of yourself, of the others involved in the organizational mission, and of the environment at large.

It all becomes even more complex when one counts the many barriers to communication that we all face. In his book *How's That Again?* Roger M. D'Aprix lists five problems in communication:

- *The language itself.* The average educated adult in the United States uses about 2,000 words from day to day; the 500 words used most frequently have a total of 14,000 dictionary definitions, thus setting up many chances for misunderstanding.
- *Sender/receiver mismatch.* There are many causes of a potential mismatch of senders and receivers, including: lack of common background; different levels of interest; serious differences in viewpoint; and even the dread generation gap.
- *Interference, or "noise."* Potential problems include: distractions of all kinds; limited spans of attention; selective interpretations; and conflicting inner thoughts and emotions.
- *One-way only.* The causes here include: failure of the receiver to understand the leader's need for feedback; a chain of command that inhibits the flow of information; inaccessibility of the leader; and undermining rivalries.
- *Need for overkill.* Communicators often fail to realize that messages must be constantly repeated to be understood; the sender must understand the need to be persistent, persuasive, and patient.

Attentiveness

What a wide range of options there are competing for your attention at any given time! In these circumstances, it's not easy to apply your full attention to a leadership commitment. Moreover, as a leader, your attention span should be wider and longer than the norm. Leadership is a daily trip of twenty-four hours. If you're fortunate, your followers may grant you time for rest and perhaps even other pursuits, so long as they know they can interrupt at any time and command your full attention.

How can you sort through all that you see and hear to focus on something that needs your full attention? The natural response of most people to any situation is to start with the obvious and quickly categorize what is perceived in an attempt to give it relevance and meaning. It is from the meanings we give that we form our initial responses. Usually these responses are effective if they are based upon fairly obvious assumptions.

These first reactions serve as filters for the subsequent information we pick up. If our first impression is positive, we tend to look for other positives, thus gradually building a positive view of the situation or the person. Similarly, if our initial impression is negative, we tend to look for other negatives and then come to a negative impression.

As long as our first impression is correct, we will usually be accurate in our final assessment. Unfortunately, first impressions are often incorrect. It is especially important, then, for leaders to train themselves to move beyond the obvious and to collect more specific information before coming to conclusions about a person, an action, or a situation. Otherwise, they will make heedless and needless misjudgments.

Here are three simple steps to increase your ability to attend accurately:

1. Doubt your initial impression no matter how clear it may seem to be. Ask yourself if the opposite can conceivably be true. Look for clues inconsistent with your first impression.
2. After you form your next impression, doubt it as well. Here, too, look for disconfirming information.
3. Continue using the doubting process as long as circumstances allow.

The rule of thumb here is to take any period of twenty minutes to an hour and spend the first 40 percent of the time doubting and forming different impressions. Finally, select the most plausible impression and proceed to gather information to support it.

Don't neglect your first impression. You will often feel more confident of it after considering the other alternatives. This analytical process will increase your accuracy in interpreting situations and improve your understanding of those you wish to lead. This procedure also avoids having followers feel that you make snap decisions without first listening to them.

Attentiveness and sensitivity add to the richness of your information, expand your understanding, and open you to a greater variety of responses to given situations. These qualities also prevent erroneous perceptions and make for more effective communications at all levels.

Building Rapport

Building rapport—that is, building especially close, harmonious, and sympathetic relationships—is another key element in effective communications.

Each of us has a unique style of communicating with others. And we each tend to prefer our own style and to feel less comfortable with the styles of others. This somewhat rigid attitude, this failure to build rapport, often gets in the way of effective communications. Good leaders tend to match their style of communicating, as well as their vocabulary, to the person(s) with whom they are interacting. This means paying attention to how the other party speaks—his or her rate of speech, diction, tone, rhythm, volume—and adjusting one's own speech to match.

Building rapport also means reading a person's nonverbal gestures (facial expressions, eye contact, body position) and learning to pace—reflecting or mirroring what another person does—before attempting to lead. This does not mean patronizing, parroting, or talking down to others. It does mean reflecting in one's communication not only the language but also the nonverbal presentation of the person to whom one wishes to communicate in a meaningful way.

Have you ever been very angry about one of life's little unfairnesses that came your way? Consider the following scene:

> You come back to your car in the parking lot and notice that someone has apparently opened a car door right into the side of your new little white convertible. The perpetrator has left the scene, leaving only a colored paint line of rusty blue cut into the side of your beautiful white chariot. You are livid. Just then someone returning to a beat-up Ford sedan parked two spaces away from you sees you in your agitated state and comes over to tell you to calm down and not to get excited. After all, getting all steamed up will not repair the damage, nor will it find the culprit. "Besides," the busybody continues, "that is why I never buy a new car. It would just get this same kind of treatment."
>
> What is your reaction to this advice? Obviously, this interloper has the sensitivity of the nearby brick wall. How can

someone who drives an old sedan understand anything about what you are experiencing, the inner turmoil, the frustration you feel on seeing this damage to your shiny new car?

You may eventually quiet down. You hope the insurance company will pay to have the damage repaired and not raise your rate. But this other person certainly has not established rapport with you. If anything, the person has shown a total lack of empathy with you and your situation.

What do you do when you meet angry people? Do you fan his or her intense feelings, perhaps bringing on greater frenzy? Obviously not! But neither do you want to trivialize the distress. If you wish to help and to show that you understand the person's discomfort, you had better be careful in your manner of responding.

You might start by mirroring excitement even though you do not necessarily agree or understand the reason for the anger. Certainly you can see that the person is upset—say so! Ask the person to tell you about it. Express empathy for whatever you can understand is the basis for the other's distress. After giving the person some time to vent the anger and frustration, ask what he or she plans to do about the situation.

In every encounter where you want to communicate effectively, and especially where you wish to influence another, you must build rapport. Reflect feelings. Get in touch with what that other person is really experiencing. Go beyond the words in order to understand what the person is really communicating. Get in synchrony with that person by establishing communication and, indeed, by reflecting the other's feelings and manner of communicating: That's not a bad definition of rapport!

Obviously, in building rapport to anything beyond the superficial level, you need more than just effective communications skills. You need to find the interests, values, and experiences that you have in common. But unless you get past the initial communication barrier, you will never be able to show the others how in step you are with them.

Ability to Persuade

Countless articles and books have been written about persuasive communication—presumably some good, some bad, some contradictory. We do suggest four qualities that we have found to be vitally important in establishing credibility as a persuader:

1. *Goodwill and fairness.* These qualities are so fundamental to persuasion that it hardly seems necessary to identify them here. But sometimes it's useful to point out the obvious: that our credibility builds when we show concern for another's best interests. We need to do little more than gently convey such a concern. But it must be a genuinely honest expression.

Our reflection of such goodwill usually assumes that others are similarly concerned about us and our welfare—not that the others are completely selfless, but rather that they are willing to exchange mutual good faith.

2. *Expertise.* How do you establish solid credentials with others? Should you attempt to impress them with, say, your wide acquaintanceship or with your travel? Should you mention your many important activities? . . how busy you are? . . or who might be depending upon you?

Of course not. Such tactics only call attention to yourself and ignore the needs of others. The best way to establish solid credentials with others is simply to ask questions and to listen to the answers. When you follow through and ask subsidiary questions based upon the answers, you show not only that you understand what the other person is sharing but also that you have either had some experience or gained some knowledge relevant to his needs.

Of course, you may mention along the way how you know what you know about the subjects in question. But if you are not asked, you must have sufficient self-confidence and control not to force your perceptions upon others. By asking questions and listening, then, you learn what is important and you can demonstrate that the points expressed are genuinely important to you, too. An added benefit is that, in the process, the other's perception of your knowledge and experience—if you will, your expertise—is enhanced.

3. *Prestige.* We tend to be influenced by those who have achieved a pronounced level of power. Status can be a glittery factor in one's ability to persuade others. But let us step back from this prevalent phenomenon and recognize that the real basis for successful persuasion is a person's overall long-term record of effectiveness.

While it's only natural that we tend to confer a measure of prestige upon someone who has accomplished a noteworthy objective, we must be mindful that our own attainment of prestige must be earned patiently over time.

4. *Self-Presentation.* The fourth factor related to your credibility is how you present yourself—the personal attributes you naturally display when interacting with others. These qualities include verbal

skills, a dynamic energy level, and, most of all, an unmistakable and calm projection of complete self-confidence.

Recall the last time you asked people for directions. If they seemed hesitant or unsure of themselves, your probably discarded their directions altogether and sought alternate advice. Persuasion clearly rests squarely upon our perception of would-be persuaders and how they choose to present themselves. Accordingly, you cannot aspire to communicate persuasively until you have critically and objectively examined just how you routinely present yourself to others. Such self-assessments must be made at odd intervals, almost at random, rather than on a contrived (dress rehearsal) basis.

Memorization

None of the communications literature with which we are familiar deals with cultivating a reliable memory. Yet, we are convinced that this is a crucial element in gaining credibility as a communicator and as a leader.

Perhaps the initial fact to realize concerning memory is that there are two basic elements that determine and ultimately control a person's power to retain and retrieve detail at will: (1) hereditary tendencies and (2) conscious efforts to develop and improve. Most recognized authorities on memory are in accord that the latter is, by far, the stronger factor.

There are numerous excellent short courses, pocket guides, tapes, and extended programs that can help you develop a better memory. Such improvement generally comes rapidly, but its degree and permanence are directly related to the level of your desire and ongoing determination.

A leader with excellent communications skills and a superior memory will outperform by a wide margin another leader with excellent communications skills and only an inferior memory. For validation of this claim, you need look no further than your own personal experience.

Think, if you will, of a leader who thoroughly earned your allegiance as a follower in the past. We suspect you can confirm that, unless circumstances made it impossible, this leader not only made it a point to learn the names of your spouse and children, perhaps even your date of birth and other personal data, but also remembered this information and made use of it at the appropriate times. Such a leader makes you feel cared about.

There's no doubt that a superior memory is a vital tool in the art of persuasion; indeed, it should be an early and relentless objective of the potential leader.

The Three Big Elements

In *How to Build Your Memory Power*, Professor Robin L. West of the University of Florida points out that most memory activities involve three steps: encoding, or putting information into memory; storage, or retaining it; and retrieval, or accurately recalling an item already in memory.

1. *Encoding.* The skillful communicator learns early that the first step in memorization is to form a habit of asking the silent question all day long, "Is this something I should commit to memory?"

When the answer is affirmative, close attention becomes the prerequisite to success. The principal enemy here will be unexpected interruptions and distractions. Most of these can be handled by fiercely ignoring them, but if that's not practical, either make a note to yourself to return as soon as possible to the prime subject, or perhaps leave the papers or some object on your desk in an unusual manner, as a reminder later.

The act of successful encoding them becomes a matter of reducing the desired data to a familiar form, group, or category. Perhaps you will be able to take the first letters of a key word to form a code word or acronym. For example, a word processor might have three characteristics that aid in correcting mistakes: clear correction tape (remember as C), a backspacing correction key that works automatically (A), and one line of memory (M). So, you remember the correcting process by the acronym CAM.

2. *Storage.* The more conventional method of memory storage is through association. One form of association is referred to as *pegging,* which involves "hanging" the new data on a "peg" of information that is already part of one's memory. Another method involves *picturing,* or visualizing the new data in a realistic setting or panorama that is already part of one's memory. Still another method is *chaining,* which involves seeing several pieces of new data linked together in a configuration so unusual that it is unforgettable.

Creating meaningful associations between the details you wish to retain and the knowledge you already have is the sine qua non of storage in the skill of memorization. In popular books on memory, such imagery is discussed more than any other strategy.

Another effective memory technique is the image-name match method, which is used to recall names and faces. With this method, the individual first identifies a prominent facial feature, then associates the individual's name with an object, and finally links the two together in an imagined picture. With practice, this method works remarkably well.

3. *Retrieving.* Ready retrieval is a matter of having cues plus resourceful creativity.

Perhaps some cues are built in, as in the case of the "pegs" and the associated imagery discussed earlier. Even if you have no retrieval aids already in place, your new awareness might enable you to generate a few of your own. Some people preserve old photographs and letters to jog their memories into recalling cherished events of the past.

One retrieval practice is known as distributed practice. When you rehearse a speech, for instance, it is better to do so for thirty minutes on five consecutive days than for one session of two and a half consecutive hours. Also, it is a good idea to give more time to the portions you know least well. To find out where the problems are, go through the entire recitation and mark any passages you missed. This technique is also known as selective testing.

Another retrieval technique is the mind map, which is formed by writing your main topic in large block letters in the center of the page. Then you print the key ideas so that they radiate from the center, key ideas like spokes around the hub of a wheel. Finally, connect subsidiary ideas to the radials, like tree limbs to branches. Use no more than three words per radial, and for clarity use alternate colors and symbols. Mind maps are especially adaptable to note taking during lectures or meetings.

Retrieval capacity can also be enhanced by the simple device of deciding constantly what you do *not* need to remember and thereby uncluttering the memory storehouse.

As one grows older, ready retrieval generally calls for intensified use of these and other memory strategies. Not all aspects of memory skill decline with age, but it is normal for information processing to slow down somewhat. Nonetheless, whatever age you are, you have better memory potential than you think. Work on it, develop it, trust it, and use it more.

Perhaps Tennessee Williams said it best: "Life is all memory, except for the present moment; and it goes by so quickly, you hardly catch it going." What we can take with us from this is not that memorization is a futile pursuit—not at all! The truth is that most people have difficulty harnessing their memories. But those who make the effort develop one of the most precious resources for success in communications and fostering a better understanding with followers.

Speaking

Our first advice on the subject of speaking is that those who are interested in becoming more skillful should seek professional guidance to help them master the mechanics. For now, here are our top twenty reminders of the subject:

1. For the remainder of your life, other people will form opinions of you based upon how well you speak.
2. Cultivate a well-modulated, pleasant voice.
3. Use good grammar without speech tics or twitches.
4. Having a strong vocabulary and being able to access and use it effectively can bring you increased confidence and open many doors.
5. Be aware that few speaking situations are identical. Thus, talking on the telephone, being interviewed, presenting a recommendation, running a meeting, addressing a gathering, and appearing on radio or TV each requires its own focused style and preparation.
6. What all speaking situations have in common is the necessity that you rid yourself of any and all self-consciousness. This is not always an easy task, as even the pros know, and is best approached by removing impediments rather than superimposing added mannerisms. The good news is that speech phobia is one of the easiest fears to overcome.
7. Never assume you know the subject so well that you can wing it—you will probably regret it later.
8. Prepare enough material for your allotted time. Allow about 150 words (fifteen lines) per minute.
9. Never get caught up in the charade of imitating others. Just being yourself at your best will always present your most favorable image.
10. Make your main points as soon as possible without being rude or shocking.
11. The words you speak count for much less than the spirit with which they are delivered. Aim for candor, simplicity, enthusiasm, and sincerity.

12. Keep it conversational. Wherever you are—in a boardroom, on TV or radio or in a large auditorium—imagine constantly that you are merely conversing with two or three good friends. (You might perhaps even pick out two or three in the audience and talk directly to each in rotation).

13. Rarely (if ever) raise your voice for emphasis; instead, use pauses, pitch changes, and pleasant phrasing.

14. Remember that audiences are interested first in themselves, second in people, and third in your message.

15. Avoid the enormous amount of nonsense and twaddle that has been written about delivery, the rules and rites of old-fashioned elocution.

16. Have a bright opening and a powerful conclusion, and keep them as close together as possible. Few presentations are remembered favorably for their length.

17. Let your last step in preparation be to test what you will deliver as though you are the receiver—then edit again.

18. Remember, there are no foolproof rules.

19. Put your total self into what you're saying.

20. The ability to speak effectively is one of the most gratifying of all skills. Learn it and you will savor it.

Writing

Our first advice on the subject of writing is that those who are interested in becoming more skillful should seek professional guidance to help them master the mechanics. For now, here are our top twenty reminders:

1. For the remainder of your life, other people will form opinions of you based upon how well you write.

2. Cultivate the use of good grammar, and follow the structural rules of clear writing.

3. Having a strong vocabulary and being able to access and use it effectively can bring you increased confidence and open many doors.

4. Be aware that few writing assignments are identical. Correspondence, memoranda, proposals, articles, technical reports, publications, and other forms—each requires its own style and format.

5. Most accomplished writers are constant readers, not for con-

tent alone but for greater understanding of how the language works.

6. Writing improves with practice under tutelage.
7. Good writing is the product of practice and criticism. Those who progress most are the least sensitive about changing their work.
8. Even if you find a formal outline too confining, you must at the very least organize the topics you have chosen in some logical sequence that holds interest.
9. Whatever your writing style, make it readable, precise, informative, accurate, complete, and simple, and keep it in the active voice (not passive).
10. Spontaneity is admirable, but only if you would write it that way the next morning.
11. Avoid rambling composition by delivering your main message early on.
12. Avoid stilted composition by eliminating unnecessary trivia and awkward construction.
13. If a writing assignment calls for a solution and you don't have one, defer the work until you do—otherwise the only purpose served will be to demonstrate your loquacious tendency.
14. Weed out useless words, and make the remaining ones count.
15. Do not overuse the personal pronouns I, we, us, and our in your writing. Those who do so are overemphasizing their own points of view.
16. Avoid vague generalities and habitual use of the passive voice.
17. Follow the ABCs of good writing: A for accuracy, B for brevity, and C for clarity.
18. Some believe that writing cannot be taught, only learned, because bad writing habits must be cast aside voluntarily.
19. Picture the readers for whom you are writing and think of yourself as one of them—now you're ready to edit.
20. The ability to write effectively is one of the most gratifying of all skills. Learn it and you will savor it.

Listening

In most U.S. school systems, teachers devote almost no time to helping students learn how to listen. Roger M. D'Aprix attributes this deficiency to at least two false assumptions:

1. Listening correlates positively with high intelligence. Thus someone who doesn't listen well is probably not too bright . . . and obviously you can't do much about basic intelligence.
2. Learning to read automatically teaches a person to listen.

Whatever the cause of this void in the curriculum of our young scholars, the subject of listening should not remain neglected by the aspiring leader.

The average person speaks at a rate of about 125 words per minute. Yet, most people can listen at a much higher speed. Who among us has not been guilty of filling the gaps with thoughts of our own? In this regard, two Minnesota researcher professors, Ralph Nichols and Leonard Stevens, have identified four discrete but simultaneous processes in good listening that should be going on during the gaps:

1. Anticipate where the speaker is leading the listener and what the intended end result will be.
2. Weigh the evidence used by the speaker to support major points.
3. Review and summarize the major points being made.
4. Listen between the lines to see what is being insinuated by tone of voice, gestures, and nonverbalized communication.

You must at least hear the words and discern for yourself the speaker's intended meaning, especially if the speaker is a follower on whom your effectiveness as a leader will depend. Deeds often diverge from words, so it's essential not only to hear what is said but also to understand what is meant.

If you feel that listening is just one of a bunch of desirable traits that leaders should have, please read the words and take in the meaning of Tom Peters, who wrote in *Thriving on Chaos*:

> Today's successful leaders will work diligently to engage others in their cause. Oddly enough, the best way by far to engage others is by listening—seriously listening—to them. If talking and giving orders was the administrative model of the last fifty years, listening is the model of the 1980s and beyond. . . . The listening leader inspires other leaders at all levels to be listened to. . . . to listen, per se, is the single best tool for empowering large numbers of others. . . . have the guts to ask dumb questions.

Motivation—Try "Inward Marketing"

(IM + IC = L)

Motivation was dealt with in some depth in Part Three, where there was particular emphasis on goals and participation, the "G" and "P" words. Thus, the tandem leadership principles of motivation are:

- Motivation is most effective when there are specific, predetermined goals.
- Motivation is most effective when there is group participation in predetermining such goals.

The implementation of these principles can be accomplished quite effectively through the use of our third important leadership skill, *inward marketing*. This skill is worthy of use by a leader in virtually any relationship with a group of diverse followers, in order to bring about maximum productivity of the group.

Taking the Inward Look

In the marketing of goods and services by U.S. businesses in the twentieth century, there has been a fairly rigid focus upon the needs, wants, and desires of the potential customer. Product research, cost and pricing, sales training, advertising, and all other devices available to the competent marketing executive have been linked to what the fickle customer will both require and actually buy.

This pervasive targeting of the outward distribution of goods and services on an ever-widening scale is deeply embedded in most large business organizations. We have no quarrel with it. Our concept of *inward marketing,* however, is that a major effort should also be exerted to focus on another kind of sale within the organization. These sales are not in terms of goods and services but are directed toward motivating people to do their own jobs better for their own reasons. This type of marketing links people's efforts on the job to their innermost personal objectives for individual benefit and growth.

What that means . . . how we learned about it . . . and why we are convinced of its merit are set forth here. Notice our "G" and "P" word principles throughout.

By far the most productive marketing knowledge co-author McLean ever gained was in Oklahoma City, not San Francisco where— certainly—he also learned a great deal as Director of Marketing for Bank of America, then the largest commercial bank in the world.

Soon after the occupancy of a new thirty-six floor banking home (Liberty Tower) in 1972, as Liberty emerged as Oklahoma's largest bank (up from fourth place in just thirty months), the senior staff began to enjoy considerably more visibility. In fact, it was a slow month if one or more of the top officers was not contacted by an aggressive "head hunter" offering elaborate compensation packages. Directors agreed (some reluctantly) that it was time to consider some form of bonus pay, at least for the top twenty officers. Hay Associates was very helpful, but their three-phase incentive bonus plan (Type A for individual performance, Type B for departmental performance, and Type C for the corporation's performance at the bottom line) seemed too elaborate. It was then management's strong recommendation to combine Types A and B and gear them to some very specific individual goals—"tough pars" rather than "easy bogeys"—with heavy emphasis upon business development.

In the fall of 1974, the top twenty were challenged to declare their objectives—theirs and their departments'—for 1975. The immediate reaction: "Why should I stick my neck out for an entire department . . . or even for my own performance, when so much depends upon things like the economy and the performance of others elsewhere in the bank?" But they did stick their necks out. In fact, a few fell on their noses. But even before the end of the first year, it became clear that some very real personal growth was taking place; including McLean's, as he struggled with some two dozen personal goals which he had declared along with the other nineteen officers.

Even in that first challenging year, the emphasis was on quantified goals—so that results could be measured and graded accurately at year-end. Here are a few examples (with the committed officer indicated in parentheses):

- Increase demand deposits 10 percent by introducing three new services that had already been market tested (EVP, Director of Marketing)
- Sell $10 million of capital notes in small denominations "in the lobby" (SVP, Bond Dept.)
- Increase Trust Department revenues, will appointments, living trusts, and employee benefit plans each by 15 percent (EVP, Trust Services)
- Increase service charge revenue by 9 percent (SVP, Operations)
- Develop and present to the directors a plan for their personal involvement in business development (Chairman, CEO)

In addition, of course, each of the twenty officers in the program that first year also had specific goals for making business development contacts personally, on a weekly quota basis throughout the year. This dimension eventually (eighteen months later) led to the inauguration of a completely new and different Officer Call Program for all officers (180 then, 384 now). (See the quality call questionnaire for the definitions adopted for the quality call and the quality call plus.)

The basic (board-authorized) concept was to reward both individual and team performance for quality calls as distinguished from just making a lot of cold calls simply playing the "numbers game." From the very first year, each officer was a member of a team. No one realized until much later the full effect that team peer pressure would play in the overall results obtained. Rather than mere cash awards, the marketing staff came up with an elaborate package of vacation trips which really got their attention. Later, teams would challenge each other, and the report sessions (usually a breakfast meeting of all officers) became quite eventful. When it all started in the fall of 1977, Liberty's deposits averaged approximately $700 million. During the eight years which followed, the total number of planned officer calls made during any one year has grown from 7,443 to 12,398, with annual gains in new business ranging from $22.1 million to $146.7 million. Liberty's deposits on 6-30-85 totaled $1.9 billion and Banks of Mid-America (Liberty's parent) reported total resources of $3.5 billion. The Officer Call Program—*inward marketing* at its best—has also produced some nonfinancial results not fully anticipated. I am referring to a bold new way of professional life for many of our people. Here are some examples:

QUALITY CALL
QUESTIONNAIRE

1. Did you perform research prior to making the call?

2. Did you identify a specific customer/prospect problem or need?

3. Did your call offer specific solutions to the identified problem or need?

*4. Did you call on a Liberty specialist to assist you?

*5. Did you make a "no-risk offer" to the customer?

*6. Did you make timely follow-ups?

7. Did you get results?

A Qualtiy Call Plus Will Include:

8. Have you considered what Liberty's ongoing responsibility will be once you have made this sale?

9. Have you a plan for discharging this ongoing responsibility?

10. Have you concluded how and by whom this plan will be implemented?

*may not be appropriate for every call.

- During preparation for abdominal surgery, a safe deposit officer sold his anesthetist on a money market account and later, a large CD relationship.
- A junior officer in the Controllers Division distinguished herself all year long by cross-selling IRAs and CDs to her credit card friends and graduated the next year to bringing in six-figure money market accounts.
- One of our shy operations officers skillfully converted a belligerent customer complaint into a new $300,000 CD and, as a result, is now a regular business developer.
- A central file officer, having virtually no customer contact on her job, became one of our leading cross-selling winners, simply by translating otherwise bland filing data into business development prospects.

Of course, no one of the above anecdotes would vindicate the entire program. Indeed, they are but examples of the new marketing orientation which inward marketing created for the organization. But, clearly, the entire culture of the bank had been transformed.

Banks of Mid-America certainly has no monopoly on incentive compensation. Hundreds of banks are now involved with it. What stands out most is that those officers who participated for five or more years only faintly resemble their former selves in terms of earnings consciousness, competitive edge, daring, determination, banking competence, and just plain self-confidence.

The longer we remain involved with marketing, the more convinced we become that the most successful among us will be those who help others in their organizations achieve their own individual brands of success. Marketing executives who become totally preoccupied with great touchstones like customer need, product design, cost and pricing, advertising, or sales training—each of crucial import in its own right—and fail to take the inward look at motivating those within the organization who hunger to be shown how to grow more productive, may be doomed to mediocrity and, in some cases, failure.

INWARD MARKETING PLUS INCENTIVE COMPENSATION EQUALS LEADERSHIP; that is: IM + IC = L ... The rewards of the current era in which marketing finds itself will go to those who understand this powerful, introspective concept best and already have it in place. Indeed, it is difficult to conceive of a superior motivational concept that can ever supplant it.

Inward marketing is a useful, powerful concept because it multiplies the effectiveness of followers' efforts many times over by harnessing them to each individual's personal ambitions. In time it can literally transform the culture of an entire group. $IM + IC = L$. Is this equation comparable in strength to the Einstein formula: $E = MC^2$? Perhaps not, but on a practical level, we are convinced that it is one of the most valuable tools a leader can have.

Volunteerism—the Ultimate Testimonial

At the outset, we suggested that the skill of inward marketing could be beneficial to leaders in virtually any relationship. Perhaps that seemed overdrawn. How about inward marketing in the numerous leader/follower situations where there is no financial compensation involved?

But exploring this question in relation to the volunteer world makes our case even stronger. President Bush's "thousand points of light" enormously understated the force of the millions of individuals working without pay in some civic, charitable, or humanitarian cause. What makes all of these volunteers do the incredible things they do? There are probably a million individual answers to that question. The one universal observation we can make is that people don't always do things for our reasons; yet, if it's for their reasons, we can't prevent them.

Volunteers do what they do for their own reasons and they derive their own abundant psychic compensation from doing it. Volunteerism, therefore, may be the strongest single testimonial yet for inward marketing.

Here are just a few examples of how the self-imposed principle of inward marketing rewarded these honorees of a recent Everyday Hero Survey conducted in 1990 by *Modern Maturity* magazine to identify exemplary societal volunteers:

Volunteer	*Testimonial*
• Grant Cushinberry, who operates "God's Little Half-Acre," a clothing and food give-away for the needy—Topeka, KS	"When it's a labor of love, it doesn't feel like work."
• Morris Kalmus, who has guided 500+ youths back into civilian life from Job Corps and military services—Philadelphia, PA	"You can't let George do it; do it yourself."

- Barbara Wiedner, who is a peace activist—Sacramento, CA

  "Each time I hold a new life in my arms, I understand even more clearly the purpose of my work."

- Fayola Muchow, who has devoted thirty years of her life to diverse volunteer work in developing countries—Sioux Falls, SD

  ". . . have really broadened my horizons . . . and they don't ever come back . . . just keep broadening."

- Jan Southwork, who is a literacy tutor—Bremerton, WA

  "It is heaven to see the light dawn on their faces, when they really understand."

Is It Really That Simple?

Is there nothing more involved in skillfully implementing the leadership principles of motivation than by looking inward for opportunities to link organizational objectives with the personal goals of the individuals involved? On the one hand, yes, it is that simple: Inward marketing really is a powerful concept that deserves a wholehearted and determined effort. On the other hand, there are some incentive compensation pitfalls. Following are four areas of potential problems:

1. Not all followers are primarily driven by those factors that could be classified as primarily career motivating. What about the physical, mental, social, familial, and spiritual categories? Any one of these considerations could predominate over career considerations for some participants.

2. It is difficult to make an incentive compensation plan completely equitable for all the participants; indeed, complete uniformity may be impossible to achieve. Be prepared to make good-faith adjustments to compensate for acknowledged discrepancies.

3. No process of goal setting can be infallible for very long. Unless there is provision for mid-course correction, everyone's eyes could be "on the wrong ball" for most of a year.

4. Almost any incentive plan can become a nightmare to monitor: Keep it simple.

Disraeli Nailed It

This concept of first learning what will best inspire productivity by each individual involved, then following that knowledge with accompanying incentives, presents an interesting paradox: Who is following whom?

Yet, such wisdom is centuries old. Benjamin Disraeli said it best more than two hundred years ago: "I must follow the people—am I not their leader?"

Of course from the standpoint of the follower, nothing could be more comfortable, because it's not work if nobody makes you do it. There you have the essence of inward marketing. Won't you try it?

SKILL 4

Assessment of Risk and Related Fears

(Decision Making)

Most of the trauma that accompanies assessing risks and handling fears results from either the inability or the reluctance of leaders to reach decisions. Therefore, becoming an adept decision maker in the presence of risk and fear is a leadership skill of high priority.

What happens so often is that the very presence of risk produces a rigidity in otherwise normal faculties. Few among us would be unable to walk a one-foot plank of wood, twenty feet long, lying on flat ground. But raise it twenty feet off the ground, and most people become petrified at the thought of such a walk. Why is this so?

With the plank twenty feet off the ground, the decision is a relatively easy one for two basic reasons: the reward for doing so is low, and considering the fear factor, the risk of doing so is relatively high. This example provides the direction for taking our first step toward confronting and effectively handling risk in our daily lives.

First Step: Classification of Risk

If it's relatively easy to reject taking high risks accompanied by low reward, is arriving at a decision in this area simply a matter of evaluating the risk/reward trade-off? In order to analyze this relationship, look at the two elements, risk and reward, expressed as axes perpendicular to each other in Figure 11.

On this risk/reward grid, it's easy to see that low risks offering

Figure 11.   Risk/reward grid.

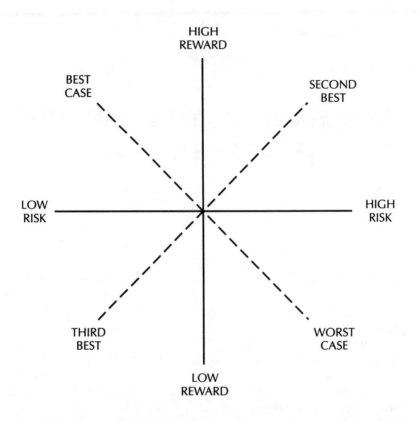

high reward (upper-left quadrant) represent the best case; conversely, high risks offering low reward (lower-right quadrant) are the worst case. Similarly, while some might argue for reversing them, the upper-right quadrant is second best, the lower left quadrant, third best.

While many subsidiary questions can be involved in the final process of evaluating risks, what we have here is an admittedly simplistic screen for determining—merely as a first step—whether a particular risk is the best case, the worst case, or something in between. For example, let's say you're the athletic director of a state university, strongly focused on your teams' win/loss records. This year, the basketball team is talented enough to be named one of the top ten teams in the nation, provided the win/loss record holds up—no more than four losses. One of your opponents has been forced to cancel a game scheduled to be played in six weeks. You have four alternatives to fill this hole in your schedule:

(a) An inferior opponent on national TV
(b) A superior opponent on national TV
(c) An evenly matched opponent on national TV
(d) An evenly matched opponent not on national TV

Clearly, in terms of risk alone, (a) is best case, (b) is worst case, (c) is probably second best, and (d) is thus third best. With ample allowance for other considerations, such as travel expense and other priorities near the open date, this problem offers an illustration of how daily risk alternatives can sometimes be conveniently and quickly classified by means of the risk/reward grid.

Second Step: Identify Related Fears

In Part One, Myth Twelve, we identified some of the typical fears that produce insecurity in the confrontation of risk:

- Fear of failure
- Fear of embarrassment
- Fear of disappointing others
- Fear of resentment

Upon reflection, each of these is but another form of fearing the consequences of making a wrong decision. So, here again, the decision is the pivotal issue. But it's virtually impossible to be decisive when one is plagued by vague anxieties. Turning these anxieties into specific fears that can be addressed, reduced, or eliminated entirely is the only acceptable approach.

For example, what is the best course of action when your sleep is disturbed by the buzz of a mosquito in the dark? The answer is to turn on the light, find the pest, and deal with it! So it is with related fears. Put a spotlight on them and deal with them one at a time. Dealing with them can range all the way from casting aside the absurd ones to recognizing that the legitimate ones may cause you to make a more conservative decision about the risk you are considering. Whatever the outcome, confronting your fears one way or the other is necessary before proceeding to the third and fourth steps.

The knowledge that you are now capable of recognizing and focusing upon fear in this manner is the key to allowing yourself to take potentially rewarding risks.

Third Step: Adopt a No-Lose Mentality

Plain logic tells us that there are three principal ways of reacting to problems: You can attack, retreat, or stand pat. Any one of these three choices may be right for a given situation. But leaders who invariably make the same choice each time are stuck in a rut that will get them nowhere. It is thus important that you think pragmatically and consider all three avenues as open each time a decision is required.

We shall take up problem solving as such in Skill Five, but it's important here to acknowledge that one's mental frame of mind has a strong influence on how a choice is made. The best frame of mind for making a decision, we believe, is the "no-lose" mentality. The pragmatist can benefit enormously from cultivating the no-lose mentality. The alternative is confusion. And that's OK, too, but only until it can be dealt with. Confusion introduces us to ourselves.

Concerning the no-lose mentality, Susan Jeffers offers two helpful models for making it happen (see Figure 12). In her book Dr. Jeffers explains her models:

> Suppose you are at a choice point in life. If you are like most of us, you have been taught to use the no-win model as you think about the decision to be made. . . . Your heart is heavy about the choice you have to make . . . should I do this or should I do that? . . . You try to take control of outside forces . . . impossible. . . . Often, after the decision is made, the no-win model makes you constantly reassess the situation, hoping you didn't make a mistake . . . berating yourself with "If only I had. . . ." You make yourself miserable . . . even when at first it seems to work out right, you already are worried that the situation may reverse itself and ultimately prove to be wrong. . . . Crazy, isn't it!
>
> Go back and stand at the choice point again. . . . Notice that two paths lie ahead—A and B—both of which are right! . . . Each yields nothing but benefits . . . clearly a no-lose situation . . . despite the outcome. . . . There are those who really think this way—and their approach to life is a joy to be around!"

Dr. Jeffers also notes that she usually encounters skepticism when introducing the no-lose model for the first time. But she invariably convinces her students and/or clients that, using the no-lose ap-

Figure 12. Risk/choice models.

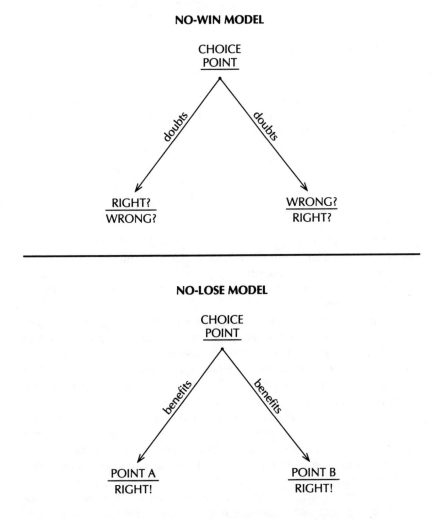

NO-WIN MODEL

CHOICE
POINT

doubts   *doubts*

RIGHT?   WRONG?
WRONG?   RIGHT?

NO-LOSE MODEL

CHOICE
POINT

benefits   *benefits*

POINT A   POINT B
RIGHT!   RIGHT!

*Susan Jeffers, Ph.D., *Feel the Fear and Do It Anyway* (New York: Fawcett Columbine, 1987), pp. 112–113. Reprinted with permission of Harcourt Brace Jovanovich.

proach, what might have appeared to be a loss is really a new opportunity to make adjustments and set up new dynamics for winning.

Fourth Step: The Dual Decision

In normal progression, the fourth step might simply be to make the basic decision and get on with it. Instead, we submit that where risk and fear are concerned there are really two decisions to make, and the first is almost useless without the second. Indeed, for best results, the decisions must be made simultaneously. Here is the pattern of the dual decision:

1. To make the basic decision on time
2. To get ready to cope with unexpected problems

Failures, duly recognized, can be good friends and wonderful teachers. Even fear of failure can be a powerful motivator for those who are prepared to make the adjustments necessary to cope with unexpected problems. (Coping can mean either solving or adapting to such problems.)

Thus, just as crucial as making basic decisions in a forthright manner is the companion decision each time to condition oneself to expect, accept, and adjust to the unexpected. People who get on in this world find the right circumstances for themselves . . . and if they can't find them, they make them. For comparatively few decisions are simple, cut and dried, leading to predictable results.

In his 1966 book *The Effective Executive*, Peter Drucker proclaimed that, in fact, a decision is "rarely a choice between right and wrong . . . it is at best a choice between 'almost right' and 'probably wrong' . . . but, much more often, a choice between two courses of action neither of which is probably more nearly right than the other."

Another important fact to be aware of is that few big decisions are made by acclamation on the part of those most interested in the outcome. In fact, the man who built General Motors, Alfred P. Sloan, is reported to have said at a meeting of one of his top committees: "Gentlemen, I take it we are all in complete agreement on this decision." Everyone around the table nodded assent. "Then," he continued, "I propose we postpone further discussion on this matter until our next meeting to give ourselves time to develop disagreement and thereby gain some understanding of what our decision is really all about."

The dual decision is meaningless unless you genuinely mean to follow it and actually do so. You may need to engage in whatever self-talk works for you. One process is described in Dr. Hornell Hart's book *Autoconditioning*. It is no more complicated than finding a quiet place, totally relaxing with eyes closed, and calmly resolving to approach all things confronting you with an absence of fear in any form.

Perhaps it is more than coincidence that the Chinese word for danger is spelled the same, except for one character, as the Chinese word for opportunity.

Will you be the one character in your life who can decide to convert dangerous risks and fears into no-lose opportunities?

If so, you will have mastered our fourth leadership skill.

Unexpected Problem Solving—The MPM Revisited

(The Six Building Blocks)

The Surgery of Objectivity

In any leader/follower relationship, unanticipated problems arise. All of the subjective reactions that occur when this happens are quite natural and necessary. However, in our view, it is in their objective responses that the leader and group will find satisfactory solutions.

The sad thing is that objectivity is not a natural human trait. Most of us must consciously cultivate and nurture it. Even then, unless we are sufficiently disciplined to remain on guard at all times, it is distinctly possible that we may try to solve unexpected problems with less than complete objectivity.

Indeed, for some very intelligent and productive people whom we know, eliminating subjectivity would require major surgery! (Hence the topic of this section.) For most people, fortunately, such surgery can be avoided by taking a full prescription of self-discipline.

Nothing can be more overwhelming than a barrage of unexpected problems. Indeed, only one unannounced development involving new risks with their added fears can create havoc. Even after you have taken all four recommended steps in Skill Four, including the final dual decision—vowing to cope with the unexpected—you still must face the matter of just how to overcome a challenging new difficulty. The six building blocks that follow offer one way to find a solution.

Block 1: Measure the Decision Gap

Effective leaders must be ready for any unexpected problems, determined either to solve them or to adjust to them. However, before you leap off into a sea of alternatives and thrash around with conflicting rationales, a vital preliminary building block must be put in place.

We presume the original decision to pursue a particular course of action was based on some measure of enlightened reasoning. Indeed, perhaps it was the result of following your Master Planning Model (MPM) or some adaptation of it. Thus, in the beginning, there must have been a desired objective. When such a goal is threatened and another outcome appears to be likely, it is time to put our building blocks in place.

The essence of Block 1 is to measure and, if possible, to quantify the gap, the distance between the desired objective and the likely outcome of the current course of action; hence our term, *decision gap*. It goes without saying that, if there is not a measurable decision gap, then there is no reason to proceed further with the succeeding building blocks of Skill Five.

When precise measurement of the decision gap is either impossible or impractical, we suggest that you consider four very plain approaches offered by John D. Arnold for assessing the breakdown between attainment of a desired objective and the current outlook. These four are from his 1978 book, *Make Up Your Mind:*

1. Something is wrong and needs to be corrected.
2. Something is threatening and needs to be prevented.
3. Something is inviting and needs to be accepted.
4. Something is missing and needs to be provided.

Once the leader has been able to give definition and/or understanding to the decision gap, it is time to put Block Two in place.

Block 2: Return to Research

In trying to close the gap between original expectations and currently projected outcome, the second building block, Return to Research, should be of help. The first element of the research should be the gap itself. How wide it is will, in fact, be a good measure to use in revalidating and/or faulting the original research objectively.

In the Master Planning Model, we proposed four forms of research: economic, market, organizational, and other. These formed the basis for adopting certain objectives, that is, goal setting.

There are many possible causes for a decision gap. Perhaps the original research was faulty, or the goals were too ambitious, or the planning process was flawed, or the implementation simply was not carried out skillfully, or the monitoring of results was riddled with inaccuracy. Perhaps a combination of two or more of these factors or of others not mentioned here is at the heart of the problem.

To begin an adjustment systematically with any confidence in the outcome, the leader should thus return to the original research and look carefully for any faulty analysis that may have occurred. Was the assessment of the economic outlook wide of the mark? Were competitive pressures in the marketplace underestimated? Were organizational talents misjudged? Each of these is a business-related example of what can go wrong, but they are useful analogues for various non-business problem areas as well.

Block 3: Rethink the Goal(s)

When previously adopted objectives are either too vague or unrealistic, there can be no better time than now to reconsider them. It may well be that the leader or perhaps some overzealous followers simply become too bullish concerning what could actually be done. Such exuberance must be isolated and checked—that is the intent and purpose of Block 3.

Care should be taken, of course, to avoid watering down objectives that may only appear to be misguided. The real error may lie in one or more of the four original steps activated in the MPM process.

However, until carefully restructured goals with measurable checkpoints along the way are confidently agreed upon by everyone to become involved in reaching them, the remaining building blocks will be useless.

Block 4: Make Better Plans

It may well be that the original plans were not organized according to near-term, medium-term, and long-term goals. Or perhaps that planning was based on vague ideas, generalities, or overconfidence in certain people or things.

The gap between the previous goal and where current efforts are headed cannot be closed without careful planning. Precision is paramount. Any time you are considering (or reconsidering) a plan, you should closely examine everything that can go right and everything that can go wrong.

Be reminded as well that, while planning is the MPM's centerpiece, there are two steps before (research and goal setting) and two steps after (implementation and monitoring results)—and so it is with replanning.

Block 5: Reinforce Implemetation

All of the renewed research, goal setting, and planning under the sun will go for naught unless firm decisions are made about *who* will do *what* and *when*. When a crisis arises, whatever excuses are given, the fact is that much of the time someone has failed to perform as planned.

As in many group relationships, when there are multiple rivalries and personalities involved, there is the natural tendency to function in such a way that all backsides are covered at all times. It is not easy for the leader to penetrate this maze of defenses. But solving unexpected problems demands that it be done quickly and fairly. How the leader conducts such inquiry and resolves the problem while protecting vulnerable personalities from undue humiliation is a key to enlightened leadership.

Care should be taken in the reinforcement process to provide backup systems where none existed before. With only a limited staff, this may not be possible without great risk of fatigue and resultant neglect of some duties. But exposure to these is preferable to poor reinforcement.

Block 6: Grade Interim Results

One of the most costly failures of all is lack of timely measurement of the results of group activity. A lag in this process often means that the more pressing priorities of the present will overwhelm the findings about the past. When it's all ancient history, the leader's responsibility to rally a renewed effort to do better is made all the more difficult.

Here's a glimpse of the six Blocks in sequence:

Block 6: Grade interim results
Block 5: Reinforce implementation
Block 4: Make better plans
Block 3: Rethink the goals
Block 2: Return to research
Block 1: Measure the decision gap

When results are found to be well short of original goals and the unexpected problems have erupted, one immediate step can usually be taken: Address measurable checkpoints along the remainder of the way, as proposed in Block 3, and grade them strictly. Obviously, interim results will be impossible to monitor in Block 6 unless measurable checkpoints were adopted in Block 3. A more sensitive scorecard can do wonders in terms of shortening response time, the real key to coping with unexpected problems.

Objectivity Through Simulation

The leader must maintain complete objectivity at each level. To test this objectivity, here are five "upset" questions from James K. Van Fleet's book *The 22 Biggest Mistakes Managers Make and How To Correct Them.*

1. Am I just *assuming* something to be true?
2. Do the facts verify my assumption?
3. Is wishful thinking getting in the way?
4. Am I confusing chance with cause and effect?
5. Will my hunches pass the test of logic?

Leaders know that no one consistently solves problems—whether unexpected or expected—without a base of knowledge. Accomplished problem solvers often simulate possible problems in their mind's eye during their spare time.

Such a pastime has no doubt contributed to the what-if technique of problem solving. The idea behind such simulation is to remove oneself from all subjective influences by posing a series of question like:

- What if we introduced this new customer service in our headquarters city only?
- What if we introduced the same service in four cities simultaneously?

Follow-on what-if questions would deal with such variables as cost and pricing, sales training, advertising, sales volume, and customer research. This is one way an objective knowledge base can be validated and tested through simulation rather than from costly trial and error.

From the University of Wisconsin (through the Extension Division and Professor Robert Clauson), a series of fascinating tapes are available for introducing simulated problem solving at the grade school level.

The MPM Revisited

Please take a closer final look at Blocks 2 through 6. See anything familiar? Blocks 2 through 6 are identical to Columns I through V of our Master Planning Model (MPM) presented in Leadership Principle 5 (Figure 7).

When unexpected problems clamour for solution—once the decision gap has been measured objectively (Block 1)—we have found that a return to Research, Goal-Setting, Planning, Implementation and Monitoring Results (the MPM) can yield genuine solutions.

SKILL 6

Relationship Renewal

When differences or, perhaps more often, misunderstandings occur between friends or fellow workers, well-established relationships can become strained and sometimes be driven to the breaking point. When strain turns to resentment or bitterness, the relationship can be said to be severed. Poor relations between followers can be as crucial to the final outcome of a group effort as breaks that involve the leader directly.

Enlightened leaders need not be daunted by this phenomenon because not all such breaks are necessarily terminal. Indeed, a carefully nurtured fracture can become a point of strength for the future. It is therefore incumbent upon the leader to be highly sensitive to any manifestations of conflict and to try to heal any breaches.

Handling Conflict

In the ancient words of Publius Syrus, "Anyone can hold the helm when the sea is calm." While the building of enduring relationships is a leadership imperative, the inevitability of conflict must be acknowledged.

Few human relationships are immune to conflict. Awareness of the ever-present potential for trouble and how to prevent and/or deal with it when it comes is like pure gold to those who would lead. Such knowledge will be useful not only in the leader's own personal dealings with others but also in the leader's efforts to observe and intervene positively in any outbreaks of conflict among the followers.

Causes of conflict are plentiful. Many seem to be rooted in personality differences, which immediately calls to mind the Wilson Grid in Part Three (Principle 1): drivers, expressives, amiables, and analysts. The inference here is that such differences can result in conflict. And so they may. But also be aware that conflicts may occur readily between occupants of the same quadrant.

Other conflicts are rooted in organizational differences. Sometimes the structure of an organization can almost automatically pit one group against another. For instance, just let the prestige of one department rise above that of another and watch the expressions of the rivals as they pass in the corridor. Still other conflicts arise from what we shall call symbolic differences. The location of an office, even the size of a desk, can produce conflicts of the most disruptive sort.

Obviously, a good many problems in relationships result from substantive differences. There are honest-to-goodness variances in points of view that go to the very core of people's psyches, testing their intellectual resolve and patience as they try to work out those legitimate differences of opinion for which most of us don't always leave room.

There are a great many methods for handling conflict, including the following:

- *Ignore it.* One might just say, "It's been a bad day—these things should be expected—I need to move on."
- *Reject it.* One might elect to dismiss it as nothing to be concerned about: "Jack and I have a good long record of compatibility; this breach is not significant."
- *Attack it.* One might decide to move assertively to confront the other party or parties involved and shake out the difficulty; "We shouldn't let something like this bother us so much; let's rise above it."
- *Arbitrate it.* One can be assertive in a less forceful way and suggest a thorough (but not endless) discussion: "Let's see what some give-and-take can do for us."
- *Resolve it.* In the end, resolution usually requires achieving consensus on the basic differences that produced the conflict: "We have the conflict behind us now, having agreed upon what's really important here."
- *Benefit from it.* We have often observed that, when the sparks start flying, we are about to get the best out of everyone. (But careful, please: no short circuits!)

The Six-Step Method

We shall have more to say about the prevention of conflict and broken relationships in a few pages, when such preventive measures will be all the more welcome after we have described our six steps for relationship renewal:

Step 6: Performance (confidence)
Step 5: Determination (hope)
Step 4: Compromise (creativity)
Step 3: Joint reason (objectivity)
Step 2: Mutual acceptance (trust)
Step 1: Mutual respect (integrity)

It is essential to recognize that, if neither party favors the renewal of a broken relationship, the Six Steps—nay, a thousand steps—will be useless. At least one of the parties—and preferably both—must be able to visualize the positive consequences of the repair. Another necessity is orderly persistence.

Once the Six Steps have been undertaken, they become both singular and interdependent, so that each must be concluded before proceeding sequentially to the next.

Step 1: Mutual Respect (Integrity)

Anyone who has ever attempted to reconcile a broken relationship knows how futile the effort can be without some measure of respect between the parties. It has become our view that such respect can never be a reality if the integrity of either party is at issue. Since a good many broken relationships stem from what one or both estranged parties has viewed as dishonesty or insincerity, the fulfillment of Step 1 is rarely a routine undertaking.

Obviously, there is little purpose in attempting subsequent steps until a solid mutual respect can be established—and mutual respect is but a figment until each of the parties can genuinely profess a new belief in the integrity of the other. The perceptive leader must determine in his or her own way whether such apparent belief is merely affected for expedience, or if it is for real.

Step 2: Mutual Acceptance (Trust)

Belief in the integrity of the other party is essential, but it is not alone a strong enough platform to support a new relationship. There must also be a mutual desire for interpersonal involvement. We refer to this as mutual acceptance, and it cannot occur without mutual trust. As difficult as it usually is to attain mutual respect, rekindling mutual acceptance can be far more formidable than a mere step on a ladder—more like climbing a very steep mountain. At the center of mutual acceptance is trust, which is hardly an ingredient to be ladled out on demand. It is rather a core belief within each of us that we bestow on very few others. How to rekindle trust, once lost, is among the leader's greatest challenges. There are as many formulas as there are personalities involved. At this point, we can freely acknowledge that steps 1 and 2 are the most crucial of our six and, taken together, by far the most difficult to achieve.

Step 3: Joint Reason (Objectivity)

It is in Step 3 that the well-intentioned leader will discover how thoroughly Steps 1 and 2 have been taken. For there can be no joint reason between the parties until both integrity and trust are strongly in place. In this sense, Step 3 may be thought of as a test, which will play out as follows: When communications between the parties become marred by subjective emotional outbursts, the test can be said to be a failure. Joint reason cannot be the product of such dissidence.

Step 3 is all about building genuine objectivity between the parties. Then, and only then, can a process of joint reason commence—as it must in order for relationship renewal to occur.

Step 4: Compromise (Creativity)

Once genuine objectivity has contributed to joint reason between the parties, creativity can be given a chance.

Inevitably, reconstruction of a broken relationship can run into a variety of impasses. None of them need be fatal to the effort—not when there is a spirit of compromise, and this is where creativity can be of great value.

The major ingredient in compromise is a willingness to lose some of the encounters, all in behalf of winning certain others. It then becomes a matter of each participant deciding what the acceptable combination of intermediate wins and losses shall be.

When the process reaches the point of planning the outcome through creative compromise, the remaining two steps become comparatively easy to achieve.

Step 5: Determination (Hope)

All the integrity, trust, objectivity, and creativity will go for naught if there is only a halfhearted intent to complete the process.

And at this point, there can be little if any determination until there is a realistic basis of hope for a successful conclusion of it all.

It's nearly impossible to be determined about a hopeless situation. But let there be some meaningful hope for a restored relationship, and determination will flourish.

Step 6: Performance (Confidence)

From here on out, it's a matter of joint mutual performance by the parties. But performance cannot occur until hope has turned to confidence.

What a challenge! In Step 6, all else is on the line. Both parties must make it happen, and that means a strong and necessary injection of genuine mutual confidence. A pet rock we saw recently summed it up fairly well: "You never know what you can do until you try to undo what you did."

Prevention of Broken Relationships

Perhaps now it will be clearer why we have elected to address prevention after presenting our Six painstaking Steps for relationship renewal. How much easier it would be in the long run to avoid the renewal process altogether!

Few of us have so many strong relationships that we need not worry if one is lost or strained to the point where the level of shared respect or trust is threatened. But too few of us seem to know how to go about renewing a relationship gone sour.

Nearly everyone can recall a regrettable exchange, perhaps an emotional one, with a long-time friend. Or perhaps it was some basic difference of opinion that brought about the erosion of a friendship.

In either case, there is usually a pause, a quiet period in which both parties reflect upon their points of view, perhaps what each has said in a hasty exchange and what each has heard from the other. During such a pause, each has a choice to make concerning the future of the relationship. For it is at this point that the relationship can be interrupted or it can be saved before it's too late. The fragility of the relationship can be overcome, if necessary, by only one of the parties.

A pair of prolific Harvard professors, John J. Gabarro and John P. Kotter, has developed a clear-cut format for building compatible relationships and preventing fatal build-up of conflict between otherwise well-meaning parties. In their article "Managing Your Boss" in the

Harvard Business Review, they suggest that, among fallible humans, managing a compatible relationship requires:

- A good mutual understanding of each party's strengths, weaknesses, work styles, and needs
- That such knowledge be used actively to construct a healthy new work style characterized by mutual expectations which meet the most critical needs of each party's concern

Here's their checklist for guidance in managing relationships of all kinds.

- *Make sure you understand the other party's:*
  —Goals and objectives
  —Pressures
  —Strengths
  —Weaknesses
  —Blind spots
  —Preferred work style
  —Preferred life style
- *Assess yourself and your needs:*
  —Your strengths
  —Your weaknesses
  —Your personal style
  —Your predisposition to lead and/or to follow
- *Develop and maintain a relationship that:*
  —Fits both parties' needs
  —Fits both parties' styles
  —Is characterized by realistic mutual expectations
  —Selectively uses the time and resources of the parties thoughtfully

What emerges here is simply that each party must buy in on the effort to prevent broken relationships. We commend the act of mutual proprietorship to any pair who desire to avoid the painstaking chore of attempting to renew a troubled relationship.

PART FIVE

Application of
Leadership Skills

(Spanning the Chasm Between Understanding and Applying Leadership Skills for Long-Term Success)

> Knowing only what to do is a country mile short of also knowing exactly how to do it.
>
> —Anonymous

In our studies of successful leaders—and, indeed, in our own experience over the years—the solid practitioners have been readily separated from the abstract theoreticians. Many times, both have been well versed on *principles* and *skills*. But what the effective ones have had that the others have lacked is the innate or acquired ability to *apply* what they have known about leading others.

It will be our purpose in this primary division of *Leadership—Magic, Myth, or Method?* to present the six approaches to effective application of leadership skills; in terms of what is needed in order not only to open negotiations with potential followers but also to foster their cohesive growth and productivity. Those approaches are:

1. Recognition of individual potential.
2. Willingness, the first component.

3. The ensuing four step process.
4. Recognizing the four general categories.
5. Applying the productivity grid.
6. Ignition—assimilation—empowerment!

But, before we proceed with these six approaches to making it all happen, we must again enter some caveats:

First—it would be absurd to claim that there are six and only six techniques for applying leadership skills;

Second—preoccupation with skills application techniques alone will fall short of achieving success as a leader.

Third—an appreciation of our proven leadership principles will be an effective catalyst (please see Part Three).

Fourth—skills application techniques will flounder in the hands of a would-be leader who is not firmly grounded in the skills themselves (please see Part Four).

In Study 5 of Part Two, we talked about the always "challenging process" of moving from "followership" to "leadership" and the teachings of some of the early leadership trait theorists. In broad perspective, we earnestly believe that the degree to which the aspiring leader masters what follows here concerning skills application will govern both how soon and how successfully followership can be left behind.

Against this backdrop, we shall move now into what is perhaps the most delicate and subtle phase of truly practicing leadership through effective skills application. As we have already suggested, techniques for spanning the chasm between merely understanding precious leadership skills and, much more importantly, methods of applying them effectively are no doubt as plentiful as there are successful leaders willing to proclaim them. At least there may be several more of such techniques than the half dozen to be examined here. But we do have strong convictions that the six which follow will serve the leader well—whether a fledgling neophyte or a veteran.

Further, while the correct choice of one or more of the Leadership Skills presented in Part Four for addressing a leadership challenge can be vital, we feel that an understanding of our recommended application techniques will be crucial to the outcome.

Recognition of Individual Potential

One of the most devastating things a leader can do to stifle results is to fail to recognize at the outset that nearly everyone has a vast potential for accomplishment. Equally guilty are those followers who fail to develop their own potential for leadership. For we contend that virtually all have the potential to lead. Let us consider how to unleash that potential.

Development of Leadership

An individual's potential to lead is never more apparent than when an amorphous group has no chosen leader or when it is being led poorly. Let's consider how this happens.

Leadership is the outgrowth of a relationship between at least two people. As this relationship is carried out, situations occur or barriers arise that inhibit or prevent those in the relationship from achieving their goals. When this occurs, someone in the relationship generally suggests a way to address the situation or to overcome the barrier. When those in the relationship act on the suggestions, we can say that leadership has occurred. If the situation is successfully handled and the barrier is overcome, we can say that the leadership was effective.

Step 1: Practice Influencing Others

The simple act of influencing another person is the fundamental building block of leadership. Virtually all of us have had this experience at some point in our lives. The more we attempt to influence others, the more likely we are to be successful in getting them to follow our lead. And the more we get others to follow our suggestions, the more opportunities we have to address situations and to overcome barriers effectively—to lead. As we learn to lead others within our relationships, they learn to look to us to lead them.

The first step toward utilizing your potential for leadership is to try to influence one or more others to accomplish something that you happen to know they want to accomplish.

Step 2: Identify Similarities Between Yourself and Others

People within relationships are alike in many ways. They tend to have similar values; to speak about issues in ways that the others understand, to have personalities that are similar to the personalities of the others who are in these relationships; to have ability levels similar to those in the group; and to be pleasant or at least agreeable.

We generally follow those who are similar to us, those with whom we can identify, and those whom we understand and trust. We are less likely to follow those who are clearly dissimilar—whether in the way they speak, or in what they seem to value, or in the approach they take to the situation in which everyone is involved.

The second step toward utilizing the potential for leadership is to understand that being a leader requires you to endeavor to become more similar to those you wish to lead, stepping out only slightly ahead of them in addressing the barrier or task that all are facing in the relationship.

Step 3: Recognize and Meet Others' Expectations

We usually like people who like being in a relationship with us. Relationships that last usually involve people whose needs are complementary to the needs of the others in the relationship. For example, one person may need to be taken care of, another may like to care for others.

Another complementary need is to expect the best from each other. The leader expects the best from the follower, and the follower has every reason to expect the best from the leader. When this does not happen, the follower or the leader is less inclined to be influenced by the person who fails to meet this expectation.

Examples are everywhere. Perhaps you have observed the consultant who talks in jargon, not in language understandable to the client, and thus fails to influence that client. Or you may have experienced the salesperson who talks down to you, a potential buyer, turning you into an erstwhile buyer; no one likes to be disparaged. Or you may have heard the public speaker who appears condescending as he or she attempts to influence an audience with flattering, high-sounding, but empty oratory. All these people and others like them fail to recognize the enormous potential of those they wish to influence.

Why do we react this way to lowered expectations about our personal capabilities? Perhaps because it is highly complimentary for another to expect the best from us. Expecting anything less puts us down or may make the other appear to be patronizing.

Rabbi Harold Kushner said it well in his bestseller, *When All You've Ever Wanted Isn't Enough*:

> We misunderstand human nature when we think we are helping people by not expecting very much of them. To be human is a great thing, and God pays us the ultimate compliment when He makes demands of us that He makes of no other living creatures. It may be hard to be good, given all the distractions and temptations of the world, but it is a lot harder to be told that you don't have what it takes to be good, so you are excused from trying.

The third step toward utilizing the potential for leadership is attempt to meet the needs or at least the expectations of those you wish to influence.

Step 4: Take and Relinquish Leader Roles

In long-lasting relationships, there tends to be an equality, a sharing of responsibility for maintaining the relationship, even a sharing of the leadership, depending upon the issues and barriers that arise. To the extent that this equality is not there, the relationship is unstable. For example, in the marriage relationship, two persons with very different skills and complementary needs may get together and contribute in unique ways to each other. In this way, many different barriers and tasks are addressed successfully, and leadership in the relationship shifts back and forth between the wife and husband.

In volunteer organizations, where membership is strictly by choice, we can sometimes observe the pitfalls of poor leadership. If one person always seems to be directing, then the others may feel that they are simply extensions of that person. Such a leader begins to feel that only he or she is really able to handle the important activities. Generally, the consequences of such behavior are reduced attendance and a lack of enthusiasm on the part of those who do attend. Ultimately, even the leader feels overburdened and burned out, finally resigning because no one else in the organization really cares. How sad!

It is unrealistic, even highly egotistical, for one person to expect to be the fount of all wisdom in a group of adults. The failure to empower others is a form of betrayal by the leader of those who follow. In a successful adult relationship, it is unrealistic to expect one person to know how to address every situation and barrier. Leadership, therefore, must shift from one person to another. In this way, everyone may experience the role of leader and thus feel a sense of responsibility for maintaining a satisfying relationship.

In the guerrilla wars we all encounter in the battle of life, there are times when everyone must lead. Leadership, then, is the product of a relationship that provides sufficient support for one (and more!) in the relationship to attempt to affect how the group will accomplish its desired goals. If the leader is successful, then he or she is very likely to attempt to lead in the future.

The fourth step in attempting to utilize the potential you have for leadership is to expect to take and then relinquish leadership depending upon the situation and the needs of those in the relationship. Otherwise, you may find the task too awesome to accept or you will burn out, as you attempt to do more than is reasonable for one person to accomplish, meanwhile failing to acknowledge the potential of the others in the relationship.

Step 5: Support Each Other

In some relationships, you may lead but be unsuccessful in accomplishing a task. Or you may experience only limited success. In such circumstances, you may be tempted to see yourself as a failure. Instead, you must learn to appreciate the support of the others who tried to do things your way. Precisely because of your followers' support, you are likely to try again. Sensitive leaders are solicitous of others' views and will carefully consider all suggestions, implementing them if possible.

A "failed" leader who has followed the suggestions of the group—or at least has given them serious consideration—has learned a valuable lesson: Group involvement and participation in directing the group makes those in the relationship more cohesive and contributes to their taking collective responsibility for the outcome. This is particularly true if the group is supportive and happens whether or not the group's goals are met. In some cases, the leader may continue in that role; otherwise, another may take over leadership.

The fifth step toward utilizing the potential you have for leadership is to observe how supportive those in the relationship are of each other. The more supportive the relationship, the more support a leader will receive and, in turn, the more support the others will expect from the leader.

Step 6: Know Your Worth

The phrase "support the others" means that those in the relationship are willing to listen to each other and to consider seriously everyone's thoughts and ideas. In cohesive groups, praise as well as criticism of one another's actions can be given. This kind of give-and-take demands that those in the group have acceptable levels of self-esteem.

Self-esteem tends to have a major influence over how much a person will utilize his or her potential to lead others. As we have said before, leaders will inevitably fail in some of their attempts to help the group succeed. Leaders with low self-esteem may be deterred from reaching their goals by self-criticism or criticism from others. The more influenced a person is by criticism, the more reassurance that person will require. The ability to handle personal criticism is directly related to a person's self-concept.

We believe that a lack of self-esteem is an important underlying cause for the failure of many to step forward to accept the mantle of leadership. When you suggest to some other(s) a particular way to approach a situation or address a problem, you accept the risk that the suggestion may not be accepted and may even be incorrect.

If you have a fragile self-image, you may tend to magnify a trivial mistake into a cosmic personal defeat. You may see the mistake as a sign that you have some major personal defect and that, therefore, you lack value or worth. Low self-esteem is, to a great degree, a fear of being rejected personally.

We cannot here address the underlying problems of those who have a neurotically poor self-image; that is the domain of those who treat psychological disorders. But we can suggest to those who are confident enough to want to lead but who need some help and encouragement, that there are ways to begin the process of building self-esteem. In our sixth step, we propose a modification of some of the principles suggested by David D. Burns in his book *Feeling Good*.

The sixth step in attempting to utilize your potential for leadership is to confirm and know your own worth:
First, when negative thoughts occur about leading the group, don't continue to let them prey on your mind. Instead, write them down and read them back to yourself to see if there is any merit to them. These thoughts usually contain distortions and twisted logic, with fears all out of proportion to reality.
Second, write out a substitute statement for the distorted one you previously wrote down. Make this statement more objective, and write it so that it affirms you and contradicts the negative statement you initially wrote.
Third, read your affirming statement and then think about how to succeed in influencing the others in the relationship.

This discussion of the embryonic development of leadership behavior is summed up in the following diagram of the six steps that you can use to fulfill your potential to lead in a situation that is perceived to be sufficiently supportive:

Step 6: Know your worth.
Step 5: Provide support for each other.
Step 4: Take and relinquish leader roles.
Step 3: Recognize and meet the expectations of others.
Step 2: Identify the similarities between yourself and others.
Step 1: Practice influencing others.

Situational Impact: A Summary Analogy

Perhaps the analogy of the effect of pond size on the growth of goldfish may be helpful in explaining why everyone has the potential to lead in a given environment. Those who have observed goldfish know that the size of the pond in which they live tends to influence the size to which the fish grow. There are good reasons for this, including the availability of food and oxygen in the water, swimming room, and competition from other fish in the pond.

Because of these environmental factors, big fish do not do well in small ponds. They cannot meet their own needs without taking away from the others in the pond. Therefore, "being a big fish in a small pond" is an unstable situation and suggests that a big fish will have to migrate to a larger pond if it is to continue to survive and grow. The leader in a small pond thus will probably remain a small fish.

So it is with people. Those who would lead, who have grand ideas that require a lot more resources than are present where they are, will have to find ways to change their current situation, or find a new situation that meets their needs as well as the needs of those that choose to follow their lead.

But the analogy of the fish in the pond also holds several other implications about who will be leader. In a large pond where there are many large fish, the small fish will have fewer opportunities to lead. (The small fish may be a leader, however, of other small fish in that pond.) Further, in a large pond, there are likely to be many large fish that attempt to influence events in the pond. Again the analogy holds for the exercise of human leadership. Environmental factors will have a significant influence on a person's choices about engaging in leadership activity.

Here is a summary of the positive lessons for exercising your potential for leadership gleaned from the pond size analogy:

1. If you are a small fish in a large pond:
   a. Find a school of small (similar) fish.
   b. Find at least one other to influence so you can develop your leadership skills as you grow to fit the size pond you are in.
   c. Become a student of a larger fish leader, thus learning from a successful role model as you grow to fit the pond.
2. If you are a big fish in a small pond:
   a. Find ways to make the pond bigger or lead the others to a larger pond.
   b. Move to a larger pond with greater resources and larger fish and make a bigger splash.

All of this culminates in a statement about the importance of recognizing the impact of the situation on leadership action.

Realistically look at the situation in which you find yourself. What are you able to contribute to this situation? Will your ideas measure up to the ideas of others?

What is needed here is another generous measure of the "surgery of objectivity" advocated earlier. Few, if any of us, are able—without enormous conscious discipline—to set aside subjective considerations. Yet, to be able to recognize and assess accurately the full individual potential in ourselves and others is a leadership imperative.

The First Action Step Is Willingness

Once you recognize that you do have the potential to lead, you have to be willing to step forward to accept the responsibility of leadership. This requires you to want to lead. It is a volitional thing, something that comes from within. Without the desire to lead, none of what we have been describing will be of value to you.

A Thought on Unwillingness

Marketing people talk about forces that "push" or "pull" people toward changing their preferences about some product or service. These discussions derive their theoretical support from the work of the German-American Gestalt psychologist Kurt Lewin, who described these tendencies in what he called a force-field analysis. He indicated that there were driving forces, which operate to move a person toward change, and restraining forces, which act as barriers to changing behavior.

If you're going to be successful in changing your own behavior or the behavior of others, you must understand that there has to be a compelling reason for the change. We all prefer the familiar to the unfamiliar, even if the unfamiliar promises to be better than the current situation. The forces that we feel within us and from outside are strongly inertial.

Although it is not necessary to have a crisis or great pain in order to overcome inertia and to act, there is no question that pain or crisis do impel us toward acting, with adrenaline providing strong internal chemical support for the action, at least in the short term. Whether a crisis is financial or personal or some clear and present physical danger, it can move us to change our behavior. In some cases, this may mean accepting a leadership challenge.

We perceive a danger here, however. Leading is a long-term venture. If you respond to the exigencies of a particular crisis situation and accept leadership, what happens when the crisis passes? If the pressure is withdrawn and the need and/or reward for leadership disappears, will you then withdraw?

We believe that in order to make the experience of leadership personally satisfying, you need something more than just negative pressures. You need some compelling "pull" component, a positive incentive, too. Otherwise, the pressures and demands of leading will leave you less than satisfied.

There are several driving forces and restraining forces that influence a person's willingness to lead.

Societal Upheaval—A Restraining Force

In Part One, we described twelve excuses for not wishing to take the bold step toward assuming leadership. At the root of all these myths is a fear of change or perhaps a kind of complacency about the way our current activities are being directed. There is a degree of personal uncertainty, too; a lack of self-assurance. We think this latter characteristic has some foundation in the upheavals occurring in modern society.

Most of the world today is continuing to experience enormous, rapid, and fundamental change. These changes are impacting the fundamental, supporting institutions of American culture. Alvin Toffler has described many of these events in *Powershift*, the third book of his trilogy on change.

In part, these changes are occurring because of dramatic shifts in the academic preparation of those in the work force. Even though there are still many Americans who are functionally illiterate, it is nevertheless a fact that more employed people have attended college than have not attended. This better-educated group has come to expect less-authoritarian direction and greater opportunities for individual initiatives. What the popular press has called the "me" generation has effectively taken over our social institutions (family, church, government), sweeping them along in the current of social change.

Because of the lack of direction from these anchor institutions, many people are developing their own individualistic values. Despite some conservative backlash, Americans are becoming more accepting of those with different values and lifestyles. Today, finding work means finding a career; it is more than simply taking a job with the best salary and hours. Consistent with the changing nature of work and life patterns, we are emerging from the authority-oriented view of life.

As the anchor institutions have failed to provide guidelines for these turbulent times, people have responded by substituting the principle of personal responsibility as the touchstone for identifying appropriate action. This position was dramatically brought to the fore at the Nuremberg trials after the Second World War. The not-guilty pleas of the defendants, who claimed that they acted under authority, were rejected by the international tribunal. Today, individuals use their own personal values to judge the correctness of their own as well as others' actions within society. More and more people are joining consumer movements, aligning themselves with environmental activists, and taking on the government whenever it appears to legislate morality.

Calling the Enlightened Leader—A Driving Force

How does leadership fit into this maelstrom of change? Who of sound mind would venture forward to accept leadership in such turbulent times, given the fallacious conception of leadership which demands that leaders take full responsibility for the direction of their followers and that they direct perfectly rather than simply channel participation? Isn't this part of what underlies the mythology of leadership?

The changes in today's societal environment and the growth of people's orientation toward individual initiative and direction fit right in with our call for greater voluntary leadership. A person who understands that a leader joins with those who follow, involving them in the decisions that will influence the fate of the group, will find that stepping forward to lead is not such an awesome task.

The key to success in today's world is enlightened leadership. Indeed, society's continued existence may well require it. Those who accept enlightened leadership roles will be most successful at addressing the issues and barriers that confront us.

Bootstrap Leverage and the Willingness to Lead

The old admonition to "pull yourself up by your bootstraps" is clearly understood in our individualistic culture. Take responsibility for yourself, for your present condition, and do something about it.

The principle of bootstrap leverage—the willingness to lead—comes from within. To find the motivation to accept the mantle of leadership, you need only to look within yourself. For leadership occurs in your relationships with your friends and family. Opportunities for leadership also emerge within professional associations, avocational groups, and charitable organizations. And, or course, you will often find yourself facing leadership challenges in your work groups or in supervisory or managerial positions to which you have been promoted. It is up to you to step forward and take advantage of the opportunities that are all around you.

Under what conditions do you accept the challenge? What is the wellspring from which the willingness to lead emerges? Earlier, we talked about motivation and the importance of goal setting. In this chapter, we want to talk about how you can motivate yourself and others to become willing. All of this involves bootstrap leverage, which has at least four sources: a clear sense of personal direction; a strong interest, including some curiosity, about what is happening in your present situation and what may happen in the future; a genuine acceptance of yourself, your strengths and your weaknesses; the acceptance of others and their strengths and weaknesses; and an acceptance of your personal aspirations and the aspirations of others coupled with a willingness to go public with them.

1. *A clear sense of personal direction.* It is essential to have a clear view of yourself and some understanding of what you want out of life. To accept the challenge of leadership, you need to understand where you are headed.

In Method 1, we discussed the impact of self-esteem on acceptance of our potential. Self-esteem also plays a strong role in how you direct your life. Your decision to accept challenges and strive for goals is related to how well you have responded to opportunities in the past. The more successful you believe you have been, the more personal satisfaction you will experience and the more competent you will feel. Increased feelings of competence lead you to undertake new challenges and to involve others by suggesting they join you in your activities. Getting others to join with you in collectively approaching an activity in common is leadership in action.

Interestingly, many people tend to see themselves in terms of their aspirations. The more successful they have been in accomplishing earlier goals, the higher their levels of aspiration and the more favorably they tend to see themselves. People's willingness to have others join them increases as they feel more successful, and that also works in reverse.

Having a clear perspective about your aspirations comes from having a good self-concept. The better your self-concept, the more willing you will be to evaluate your goals and aspirations critically and to assess them honestly. The more objective you are about yourself and about why you do what you do, the better you will be at communicating with others about group goals and aspirations. Being clear about your own values and about your own motives will help you to help others sort out their feelings about whatever the group jointly proposes to accomplish.

To help make yourself willing to assume leadership, we propose that you answer the following questions:

Goal Questions

- What progress do I want to make—
  —In my career?
  —With respect to my family?
  —In my personal growth?
  —With respect to my physical health?
  —In my spiritual development?

Timing Questions

- What do I want to accomplish—
  —By the end of the year?
  —By the end of three years?

2. *A strong interest, including some curiosity, about what is happening in the present situation and what will happen in the future.* Another source of people's willingness to act as leaders comes from the recognition that their fate is linked to the fate of everyone in the group. On the surface, it could appear that the strong individualistic orientation we have described as today's norm would run counter to an interest in what is happening to the entire group. However, the recognition that one's interests are linked with those of others makes the idea of a common fate simply a matter of enlightened self-interest.

A second aspect of this internal willingness to lead comes from a natural curiosity about the future and an interest in being a part of the action. New goals will often give you an opportunity to test yourself in unfamiliar ways. This curiosity about your ability to handle these new issues successfully tends to draw you into taking an enthusiastic role in influencing the group toward productive action.

To help make you aware of how your interests are linked with the interests of the group, we propose that you answer the following questions:

a. How does what I want to accomplish now fit with what others in the relationship want to accomplish now?
b. How do my expectations about the future fit with those of the others in the relationship?
c. If I do not know what they want, how can I get this information?
d. How can I improve my chances for accomplishing my goals by working with others in my group?

Working on common interests increases the common fate of both you and the others and makes everyone more willing to follow the directions of the leader.

3. *A genuine acceptance of ourselves, including both strengths and weaknesses, plus the acceptance of others and their strengths and weaknesses.* Self-acceptance increases for most of us with each personal success. Unsuccessful ventures also can become the basis for future successes for those who are willing to study and thus learn from their mistakes. Once you have established sufficient self-confidence and self-esteem, you will be able to give praise and encouragement to others and to recognize their importance to the overall success of the group. Only when you have sufficient self-acceptance can you have the kind of humility and confidence needed to appreciate the value of others and what they are contributing.

It is beyond the scope of this book to address all of the problems of those with a pathological need for approval. However, we can suggest one particular way to build your own approval of yourself. That is simply to affirm yourself to yourself with positive self-talk.

Start each day with a goal of telling yourself good things about who you are.

Begin the first day by enumerating five positive things you do in your behavior. The next day, count ten positive things that you do. The following day, increase your target to fifteen such things. Continue doing this, adding an additional five items to your count each day. At the end of the week, you will be amazed at all that you do that you approve of—and you will notice a marked improvement in your attitude about yourself.

This technique will help to break any tendency that you may have to talk yourself down. It will make you aware, on a daily basis, that you do many good things. This positive self-talk also makes you less dependent upon others for approval and more reliant on yourself.

To help you truly accept others:

Talk up yourself to yourself. When you accept yourself, you will be able to accept others and their contributions to your joint efforts for success.

4. *An acceptance of our personal aspirations and the aspirations of the others along with a willingness to go public with them.* The old story is told of the professor who asked a student midway through the semester, "What grade do you want to get in this class?" The student replied, "That's a 'no-brainer,' Prof, I want an A." The professor then realized he had asked the wrong question. He checked again, "What grade do you expect to get in this class?" The student replied after thinking about his performance to that point in the semester, the amount of time left in which to change his performance, and his willingness to expend energy on the class: "I guess I expect to get a C."

This little story helps us to distinguish between wishes and aspirations. Wishes are mental reveries about what it would be nice to experience. Aspirations are internal targets; they determine how we approach the external challenges we face in daily situations. Aspirations are valuable sources of motivation.

These internal targets are largely a function of our estimates of our own ability. An overly critical or overly optimistic self-assessment is likely to distort this internal targeting process. Our aspirations are related to how much effort we will expend when we work with others. Our level of aspiration for what we can accomplish in working with others is also related to our assessment of the others with whom we work.

Aspirations are variable, they change with experience. Aspiration levels often depend upon how well we have been able to accomplish what we have set out to do. The student in our earlier example would have raised his aspiration level for a grade if he had done a better job early in the semester.

Few of us have ever dared to tell others of our dreams, in part because when others have told us their dreams, we were embarrassed for them. Yet all motivated behavior is future oriented. Holding back our aspirations—being unwilling to express them—may seem to be evidence of inner strength. But we need to realize that those around us hunger to know what's on our minds for the future and desire to participate in shaping our mutual objectives.

The opposite of complacency is wanting things to improve, to get better. This is not a pathological striving for perfection but a genuine desire to make a contribution, to improve on and build on what we now have.

To help you accept your personal aspirations and the aspirations of others:

Use your wishes as "what-ifs" to help you think of possibilities, to turn your aspirations into goals with action plans, and to commit yourself openly to meet specific timetables for accomplishment.

The Importance of a Meaningful Task

During one of the mid-life crises of one of your co-authors, he was recruited by a major manufacturer of home heating and cooling thermostats. During the evening, the company recruiter extolled the virtures and the value of heat regulators. Now there is certainly no quarrel about the importance and value of this business enterprise. It was, however, a bit of a stretch for your co-author to picture himself meeting his need to find meaning in his life by accomplishing the goals of this enterprise.

Your co-author chose not to join that organization. The recruiter did not help him to picture finding meaning for himself by giving his next years to the "romance" of heat regulator manufacturing.

Without taking a long time to address this point, it is constructive to recognize that some of the goals that we strive for early in our adult years are related to fulfilling the basic needs that we all share as humans. It is after fulfilling these fundamental needs that we begin to look for impact, for doing something worthwhile, that transcends the ordinary and gives a little "zip" to our lives.

Without having something meaningful toward which we can strive, something that goes beyond making a living (as important as that is), we are less likely to be willing to act in new ways or to take on additional duties and responsibilities. Awakening to the opportunities and challenges of leadership, pursuing something a little bit special to yourself and others around you, can provide the needed incentive to move out of the ruts of routine.

Use the Four Dynamics of Leadership

Leaders respond to the same situation in different ways because they have different levels of individual experience, because there are different levels of follower experience and expectations, and because each situation has different demands.

When using the dynamic approach, first, you identify a leadership opportunity (the opportune situation); second, you look within yourself for the willingness and motivation to act (self-motivation); third, you must resolve to believe in yourself and to acknowledge that you have something to contribute (self-validation); fourth, as you act on your beliefs, you obtain the support of others (validation by others). It is this last step that is typically called leadership.

It is through these four dynamics that you put your willingness to lead into practice. Applying these four dynamics helps you to reassure yourself that you want to continue in the leadership role. For the continuing motivation to lead is related to gaining and maintaining the acceptance of those who follow.

Dynamic 1: The Opportune Situation

Successful leadership depends, first of all, upon identifying an opportunity in which to try to influence others. The opportune situation varies depending upon your experience in leading. If you have led only rarely or never, try to take your first leadership steps in relationship situations in which there are a few people who are already supportive. Start small!

If you have some successful leadership experience, a broader range of opportunities is available. This is the time to grow and to develop your leadership approach by taking advantage of an opportunity that provides you a chance to address issues about which you feel less than confident but which you feel you have a "shot at."

If you have extensive experience as a leader, you face different choices and challenges. You need to be wary of overextending yourself by accepting too many leadership opportunities—and then burning out or losing enthusiasm. As you gain experience as a leader, you need to maintain a clear understanding of your personal and professional priorities. Remember, a need is not necessarily a call to action.

Relationship Properties

Think back to our discussion of the properties of relationships and the kinds of leader actions associated with each property. When deciding if a situation offers a good opportunity to exercise leadership, you must make sure that the situation is a good fit, based on the following criteria:

1. You are perceived to be a part of the situation.
2. You understand what can and cannot be done with the consent of the others in the situation.
3. You understand what the members of the group wish to accomplish and you can operate consistent with those wishes.
4. You understand how those in the group are interconnected or involved with each other.

Once you decide to assume the mantle of leadership, you must make certain that your attempts to influence are consistent with the boundaries of the relationship as you see them. You must also ensure that your attempts to influence are consistent with what those in the group will understand, taking care not to go beyond the knowledge level of the group members. You must also make every attempt to make the goal appear within reach, even though it may require some (or all) in the group to "stretch" or to try something not previously done.

Issue Characteristics

Just as issues vary in importance, pleasantness, and novelty, so the degree of group and leader interest in handling issues also varies. Issues of lesser importance often can be handled safely by the novice leader. Other issues of greater importance or consequence probably require a leader with experience.

The nature of the issue faced also influences a potential leader's assessment of how desirable or how opportune the situation is. There are many things that can be said about selecting the opportune situation. For the purposes of this discussion, let us use the three stated characteristics (importance, pleasantness, novelty) of issues to suggest some important points a leader has to consider when selecting the opportune situation.

If you are the leader of a group that addresses mostly routine, unpleasant tasks of little importance, this should send up a warning signal. The motivation to be a part of such a relationship and, therefore, to respond to the issues within it tends to dissipate quickly.

In these situations, you must look to break the monotony by finding an important issue or a more pleasant task to intersperse with the routine "duties and responsibilities" that require high levels of personal discipline. In this way, you can make being there personally rewarding both for yourself and for the others. It is as important to manage the payoff for being there as it is to do what is there to do.

Dynamic 2: Self-Motivation

As a leader, you need to make sure that you have sufficient self-motivation and emotional involvement with the task or the activity at hand in order to see that the job gets done properly. Without this inner drive, which comes from the desire to achieve your personal goals, you will feel no passion, no zest or enthusiasm, for influencing others. A passionless, bland leader has the same capacity to lift the spirits of others as an eighteenth-century flying machine had to lift its pilot off the ground.

What makes people willing to lead? Generally, when they recognize that something has to be done and they have an idea that just might work, they take action. The motivation here comes from a sense of personal direction and an inborn curiosity.

Another element in this willingness to step out and suggest a direction for others to follow is an acceptance of yourself, including your strengths and weaknesses. A balanced self-view leads you to express ideas with the proper combination of humility and enthusiasm. This becoming combination has a direct, positive influence upon those who hear the suggestion and then must decide whether or not to follow. It is the badge of the self-motivated leader.

Confidently putting forward your ideas for others to hear and consider means that you have recognized the rights of all those involved to react in terms of their own aspirations. Further, they will consider the implications of your attempts to lead in terms of their own future activity. Each person will think of his or her likely part in the scenario you have presented, again in terms of what each aspires to do.

Leadership is built upon aspirations, our own and others'. You must therefore be willing to share your emotions about the activity in which you are attempting to lead others. In effect, you must model for those who follow by showing what their emotions can be when, together, you successfully address the issue requiring leadership.

Dynamic 3: Self-Validation

Earlier we described the basic process by which leadership acts occur. We pointed out that when others consent to follow, leadership is born; in effect, the followers have validated the leader and his or her ideas. The leader feels a surge in self-confidence: "Yes! I did it!" But along with this powerful feeling, wise leaders feel a certain amount of caution and of healthy concern not to lead the followers astray.

When your suggestions prove to be effective, you generally become more willing to offer subsequent suggestions. The feelings of self-confidence are great! You may even take additional risks to achieve more. Remember to use the Master Planning Model (MPM) described in Part Three. If you use that model property you will improve your ratio of successful to unsuccessful suggestions. And guiding others to accomplishing their own goals will always enhance your own self-validation.

Dynamic 4: Validation by Others

Isn't a large part of leadership the genuine enjoyment of handling problems that are important to you as well as others? When one or more people follow your suggestions or when you develop a plan of action together and it works, the reward is enormous. When this happens, your leadership has been accepted, your ideas have been effective. This is the fourth dynamic for application of leadership skill—validation by others.

Unfortunately, getting your ideas and suggestions validated by others is not as simple as it may appear from our discussion thus far.

Remember that the expectations for future outcomes are understood in terms of everyone's aspirations, which vary in degrees of realism.

Remember that successful leaders don't do it all by themselves. There must be involvement of others, first in agreeing to the idea, second in acting to make the idea work. If things change—if the task is perceived to be more difficult or if the task takes an unexpected turn—those involved with the leader have a chance to adjust their aspirations.

Validation by others should occur throughout the process of acting on the leader's suggestions. Timing is important. If the leader waits until the end of the process to obtain validation from others, then this validation will depend almost totally on the success of the outcome. If the outcome is less than successful, the validation from the others may be half-hearted or nonexistent.

All endings are not happy. A number of noble efforts—superbly researched, carefully planned, and carried out with everyone's agreement and cooperation—do not succeed. Failures are not necessarily the fault of the leader or of the followers. External circumstances beyond anyone's ability to foresee or cope with simply prevent success.

Lack of validation by others of a well-led venture that proved to be less successful than anticipated certainly takes away from the enjoyment of leading. It follows from all we have said to this point about empowerment that validation can and should come while the group is involved in the active process of the venture. Ultimately, this kind of validation not only brings enjoyment to the task but also supplies meaning and purpose to the lives of those involved in the activity.

Summary of Leadership Dynamics

Mountain climbing enthusiasts do not always reach the summit. The weather may change, injuries may occur. And yet, it is the climb, the fantastic views along the way, and the mastery of the process of a strenuous and often risky task that leaves the climbers with a sense of joy and feelings of satisfaction.

Others have experienced the opportunity to run for office and have found supporters with views similar to their own. This kind of support is validating along the way. Even if the candidate loses, the very process of being supported in the contest makes the effort worthwhile. That's why many losers run again—and often win. In the political process, we develop intense, highly satisfying relationships with others who see the world as we do.

Having dared to experience the four dynamics of leadership—whatever the outcome—a leader's reward can come in a wide variety of forms. Here is the way the four dynamics go together:

Dynamic 4: Validation by others
Dynamic 3: Self-validation
Dynamic 2: Self-motivation
Dynamic 1: The opportune situation

APPLICATION METHOD 4

Taking Stock of Personal Considerations

Up to this point, we have asked you to consider seriously any and all leadership opportunities as they arise. The fact that you have stayed with us this far indicates that you have some inclination to accepting such a challenge. Of course, you may still be wondering if leadership really is for you. Now that you have learned the basic leadership principles and proven skills and you know something about how to apply these skills, you may be asking yourself, "Am I personally equipped to put it all together?" The message of this book is, *you are if you want to be.*

To help you decide when to lead, we propose that you ask yourself four important collateral questions:

1. What fears are keeping me from stepping forward to lead? (*personal risk*)
2. What am I giving to life and getting from life? (*personal priorities*)
3. Am I yet wise enough to make a leadership contribution? (*personal knowledge*)
4. Am I otherwise equipped to accept the responsibility for leading others? (*personal abilities*)

Risk to the Leader

There are any number of risks for leaders. Some of these risks are related to fears from within, such as fear of failure, fear of embarrassment, fear of resentment by the current leader. Some are related to genuine concerns about being an effective leader, such as the risks involved in overcommitment or in doing a poor job. Finally, some risks are there because we respond primarily to the needs of others and do not consider our own needs. We may be afraid of disappointing others, or we may lack self-confidence or respect for current leaders. The major negative consequences of these risks are follower disillusionment and betrayal.

Disillusionment

Recall that the leader helps followers set goals that are achievable but that contain some "stretch." The risk here is overcommitment, which may be inherent in the enthusiasm of the goal-setting process. Overcommitment may also come from trying too hard to inspire a lethargic group by optimistically setting unrealistic aspirations or overly ambitious timetables. The leader must know and understand those who follow—their strengths, their weaknesses, and the likely extent of their resolve to achieve. This can be a delicate balance, but it is required if the leader is to avoid the disillusionment brought on by promising too much.

Illustrations of overpromising abound in our daily lives, from the overly optimistic delivery dates promised by volunteer workers to the United Way chairperson (who, in turn, announces an unreachable campaign goal), to the eager candidate for office who runs on an impossible platform that is never acknowledged again after the election, to the overzealous marriage proposal. But disillusionment from overpromising seems to hurt the most when it is related to one with whom we feel some closeness. Somehow our leaders shouldn't do those things! People who have experienced these feelings are often most reluctant to assume a position where they might disappoint those who are close to them. Successful leaders influence those who follow them by helping them take the necessary risks to accomplish their tasks or to surmount the barriers that stand in the way of their success. Disillusionment often comes from miscalculating those risks.

There are five factors that influence risk-taking behavior because they strongly influence how much risk those who follow are willing to take. Leaders have the ability to influence risk taking by using their knowledge of these factors to avoid a great deal of disillusionment.

Factor 1. Groups generally have a greater propensity to take risks than do individual members of the group. This, we have found, is because the responsibility for taking the action can be spread among the whole group. Therefore, leaders need to be judicious in their use of this tendency toward greater risk taking.

Factor 2. Leaders can influence how much risk is taken by changing how the risk is "framed" or presented. Making the group choose between two apparent loss situations of different magnitude, for example, is likely to result in the group's selecting the riskier alternative.

Factor 3. If the leader offers the group a choice between losing what the group already has or gaining something of greater value, depending upon the probability of success and the magnitude of the reward, those choosing will tend to act conservatively, choosing to retain what they already have.

Factor 4. The level of prior success of those in the group will also have something to do with their propensity to take risk. If those choosing to participate in the risky alternative have previously experienced success, they will perceive themselves as likely to experience success again. Therefore, they tend to be more willing to take some chances. Obviously, there are some extenuating circumstances, such as the ease of previous successes and the magnitude of the payoff. But for the most part, prior success predisposes us to accept risk. Leading a successful group requires less prodding and greater prudence in risk taking.

Factor 5. Those with a longer-term orientation—that is, those who believe that there is more time to recover from a lack of success—tend to take greater risks than those who believe that there is less time to recover. Often this factor is attributed to a group's youthfulness, but based on our experience, we do not think this characteristic is limited to the young. Again, the leader manages this perception of time and timing.

As a leader, you must understand these five factors if you are to avoid overcommitments; this is especially true if your own needs are to be fulfilled in terms of accomplishing the mission. Risk taking that leads to failure leads to a loss of confidence and then loss of trust in the leader. Disillusionment follows from the loss of trust. Regaining lost trust among followers is difficult if not impossible.

Leaders also become disillusioned. Too often, such disillusionment emerges in leaders with an apparently self-sacrificing attitude about what they are doing. On close examination, this attitude is more likely a lack of self-confidence, a lack of self-respect, or an inordinate desire to please others and therefore a fear of disappointing them.

Leaders who fail to consider their own needs as well as the needs of those being led put tremendous pressure on themselves. The "joy of selfless service" is soon dissipated as these leaders begin to feel that they are being taken for granted.

How should you as a leader integrate this information about risk and its management with all of the other things you have to consider in applying the principles and skills of leadership? Our suggestion is to reflect honestly and objectively on your experiences, both good and bad. Learning from both successes and failures is how good leaders validate their skills—and learn how to apply them better the next time.

Successes predispose us to try again and to stretch even further. Failures predispose us to reflect upon ways to improve our efforts in the future, perhaps by doing more of something to enhance the quality of what we did, or by doing less of something to avoid failure, or possibly not doing any of the same things at all.

As we indicated earlier, motivation is nearly always based on drawing of the follower(s) toward something or someone in the future. Experience is what we use for guiding this process. Risk acceptance is related to our level of aspiration, our feelings of personal security, and the level of our confidence—based upon experience— in our capacity to motivate full follower involvement.

Betrayal

If the leader is unsuccessful in motivating the followers or in correctly estimating their potential, the follower(s) may feel betrayed because they are unable to follow effectively. They cannot trust a leader they cannot follow, nor can they follow a leader they cannot trust. Lack of trust in the leader and consequent feelings of betrayal can easily cause followers, in turn, to betray the leader. Some of those who lose faith in their leader may even become subversive and mutinous.

A leader must not ask followers to betray themselves or the others in the group. There are times when you'll have to achieve a delicate balance in order to avoid this trap.

An example of this dilemma occurred when one of the authors had to decide how to respond to a need to reduce fixed expenses in a company for which he worked. This need arose because the company could not continue to grow as rapidly as its strategic plan required without some major adjustment in the expense structure. Further, the competition within the market made growth necessary to remain profitable.

The major single contributor to the company's fixed expenses was the cost of labor. A task force was assigned to find ways to reduce the organization's fixed labor costs. Those who agreed to serve on the task force were guaranteed continued employment regardless of what their recommendations were for labor cost reductions.

After a major study of all the issues, the task force recommended a reorganization that would lead to an initial reduction in personnel of ninety people. In effect, the members of the task force had voted to eliminate the positions of many of their co-workers.

Was this a reasonable thing to ask of those on this task force? How can a leader ask that some employees find ways to "betray" their co-workers? In this case, the answer was that, prior to the deliberations, the leader had committed the company to provide a "safety net" to take care of all employees. By meeting with competitors and setting up opportunities for those soon-to-be-released employees, approximately nine out of ten were placed in new jobs within two weeks, and the remainder were placed shortly thereafter.

In summary, when you present alternatives to your followers, you need to frame the choice carefully in terms of both lost opportunities and potential gains if you want to exert an appropriate influence on the group's risk-taking propensities. It will also help if you reflect upon any prior successes enjoyed in similar situations, as well as reassure the group that there will be adequate time to recover if the effort does not turn out successfully. Above all, you should never risk overcommitment in any form.

Please recall the six steps for relationship renewal when strained relationships turn to resentment and bitterness. But, even when betrayal has occurred, the enlightened leader must resist the seductions of anger, rage, and vindication and realize again that not all such breaks are terminal. Indeed, a carefully nurtured fracture can become the strongest point of strength for the future.

Personal Priorities

Few question the importance of knowing one's priorities. What we usually hear in any serious discussion of this matter is, "How do you know how to set personal priorities?" or "What does a meaningful set of personal priorities look like?" The answers require a careful look within ourselves, an assessment of our *physical* selves (our bodily activities), our *mental* or intellectual selves (which guide our actions), and our *emotional* selves (the energy by which we change and grow).

Where we spend our time provides tangible clues to our primary personal priorities. Most of us tend to favor one of these three "selves" over the others. But in achieving the vital balance of living, we learn that each of these three "selves" demands appropriate emphasis. In their book *The Inventurers: Excursions in Life and Career Renewal,* Janet Hagberg and Richard Leider suggest what happens when people tend to favor one of these more than the others.

Mind supreme: These very unemotional, unspontaneous people live in such an intellectual world that there is little fun in life. They are frightened of people and situations unless they can control them rationally. They are out of shape, physically inactive, and scoff at things that are a waste of time (unintellectual), such as doing anything with their hands!

Body supreme: These people are expert at looking good and/or persistent in doing exceptionally well at physical activities. Physical appearance or physical prowess is of primary interest. These people's lives are geared toward appearances, and they are often immature intellectually and emotionally after initial contact. They are happy only during a physical chase or challenge. As they age, they get more and more frantic.

Spirit supreme: Expert at emotion, these people are often unstable and unpredictable. Their turbulent emotions rule. They feel from moment to moment and direct their lives on the basis of whims, moving from one high to the next. They seek quick solutions to increase the effect—relationships, mind-altering chemicals, creative expression, spirituality. Their self-esteem is often low because environmental happenings dictate their self-images. They tend to get swallowed personally in events, only to emerge with less and less ability to resolve things rationally. They begin to wonder about their inability to think at all.

Based on these categories, what do your priorities look like? Are you living a balanced life? Obviously, priorities are not static. As we mature with experience, our priorities also change.

What are your priorities for your physical self? Are they related to wellness, attractiveness, or . . . ? Do you exercise daily, eat well, get sufficient sleep?

How do you stimulate your intellectual self? What do you talk about . . . read? How do you keep up on changes in your field?

What about your spiritual side? How do you lift your spirits, stimulate your appreciation of what is beautiful, give and receive loving responses to and from those close to you?

How much time you spend on each of these three areas will tell you quickly how balanced your life is. Then you can redress any imbalance you might find by resetting your priorities accordingly. This is something you must do if you aspire to apply your leadership skills effectively.

Leaders should set at least one priority for each of the three dimensions—body, mind, and spirit. Those who lead have to know what is of importance to them. In this way, they can help meet their own needs as well as the needs of those who follow. As we indicated in our discussion of risk, we can find ourselves accepting opportunities to lead which do not meet our personal needs and the result is very dissatisfying. A clear understanding of our priorities permits us to lead boldly, at least with respect to our own goals.

Two major benefits emerge from having a clear understanding of your priorities. First, becoming aware of what's important to you gives you a clear focus on what is actually happening in your life. How you feel about yourself in a situation influences how you interpret the situation in which you find yourself.

Second, being clear about your own priorities makes you more willing to follow your instincts in making choices about what to make of a new situation. Circumstances are almost always different from situation to situation, so you cannot generally repeat exactly what you did previously to achieve leadership success. You can, however, select a plan of action based on your past experience. Then, consistent with your priorities, you can use this plan to guide your initial efforts.

Consider again the earlier illustration of the coauthor's company having to reduce its workforce. No one could be sure that the decision was the correct one. However, the basic values of those who made the decision included taking care of the people in the company; that was one of the important priorities. Those employees who remained saw that the company cared about those who had to leave. Thus, they could direct their energies toward making the reorganization of the company successful without feeling anxiety about the future or guilt about the past. Looking back, this move enabled the company to grow in a different way and at a different rate than it could have before the change. This, after all, was the priority that produced the action.

It is impossible to determine if a different decision would have been better for the company. But we do know that the company's actions were consistent with its major priorities and, against that background, that the reorganization was successful.

One final thought about priorities is related to our prior discussion of motivation and to the findings of Victor Vroom concerning the payoffs from working. One of the important social motivators in the workplace is to be taken care of by others. We know that leaders whose priorities include such a caring role tend to be the most successful over the long term in gaining follower support.

Personal Knowledge

Do you ever know enough? Isn't it true that the more you know, the more you realize you need to know? But how much do you really have to know to lead successfully? Earlier in this part we discussed the need to know about risk and about individual priorities. Now we will focus on the application of leadership principles and skills. Accordingly, in this discussion of personal knowledge, we distinguish between knowledge that comes from communicating with others about their experiences and knowledge that comes from direct, hands-on experience.

Successful leaders seek to build large reservoirs of this latter kind of knowledge. The in-depth understanding that comes from real-life experience seems to give leaders an extra measure of confidence in what they suggest to followers. Successful leadership, therefore, is often less related to what you know about something and more related to what you have experienced. Of course, how you use experiential knowledge in applying leadership skills is crucial to your success.

As discussed earlier, as a leader you have to know something about the issue or task to which the group addresses itself. You also have to know about those who are in the group—their strengths and weaknesses—and be prepared to help them meet their needs. Finally, you have to know about yourself—your own needs, aspirations, goals, and fears—and what you are willing to offer to the group.

Personal knowledge, whether gained from communication or experience, can be shallow and ineffective if you are at all reticent about sharing it openly with the group. The more forthcoming you are the more willing others will be to trust, to listen, and to follow. A genuine willingness to share knowledge predisposes others to share in return, not only their knowledge but also, sometimes more importantly, their concerns. When this happens, the group's aggregate knowledge can grow into a powerful resource.

Finally, if you are going to be a successful leader, you must willingly admit to the gaps in your experience. You may know about what is being undertaken but may not have had experience in carrying out such an effort. Knowing this, others in the group have to assess the attendant risks. If they feel great uncertainty, they may offer alternatives to your suggestions for action. Or, if the group chooses to support what you have suggested, all will be aware of the possible risk involved in their actions. Often this will lead the group to more aggressive participation in implementing existing plans or in adopting better ones. Thus, one positive consequence of admitting to gaps in your experience within cohesive groups is the extra effort that such information can bring forth from the followers.

What can we conclude from this discussion of personal knowledge? First, it is better to have practical experience than theoretical knowledge about some action; second, it is wise to share openly what you know as well as what you do not know; and third, you need to get comfortable with your own knowledge and experience and thus to accept yourself as a leader who is well on the way to mastery of leadership skills application.

Personal Abilities

Given the roles a leader plays within a group, there is one thing that leaders can do to set themselves apart from all the others: Effective leaders attempt to model for their followers what they ask them to do.

There are many who can tell people what to do, and still others who can tell people why they ought to do certain things. But the enlightened leader, with an empathic sense of what followers need to know, will actually model the desired course of action by attitude and example, thus imparting precisely how to do what needs to be done.

Applying the "Productivity Grid" to Assess Followers' Potential

The Broad Perspective

When all else is in place—the principles, skills, and skills-application techniques—for more effective leadership, the time comes when the leader is both entitled and compelled to take stock of the potential productive capacity of each follower.

Indeed, such an evaluation is imperative for revalidation of the leader's own capacity for carrying out the chosen mission. We think of the quandary of the professional football coach, who tries each week to reevaluate whether or not the players on his roster have the talent and the will to produce a winning team. Such intense efforts account for some of the frantic trading of older players for younger players plus draft choices that regularly makes big news on the sports pages.

Of course, it's not so easy to trade players in other leader/follower situations. Reallocating assignments and recruiting others to the group are the more likely alternatives.

Whatever dynamics become involved, the enlightened leader must make periodic—perhaps even daily—judgments concerning both the current capacity of each follower and, much more importantly, the ultimate long-term potential of each one.

Gaining such a broad perspective is our fifth method of achieving effective application of the skills of leadership—and we propose a fairly precise technique for going about it. This technique involves using a grid, supported by application in the crucible of experience.

What One Guru Found

In 1959, Dr. Frederick Herzberg, who is now Distinguished Professor of Management at the University of Utah, and a team of researchers published the results of a comprehensive survey of the motivation of American workers. They had asked for responses to statements such as, "Think of a time when you felt exceptionally good or exceptionally bad about your job, either your present job or any other. . . . Please tell what happened.

Out of the responses to this and a series of follow-up questions, Herzberg set out to discover what makes people happy and satisfied on their jobs or unhappy and dissatisfied. In the aggregate, respondents answered in such a manner as to isolate two differend kinds of needs/desires that appear to be independent of each other.

The research team attributed findings of unhappiness and dissatisfaction to the job environment or the job context, which Herzberg labeled "hygiene factors." On the other hand, happiness and satisfaction on the job were thought to be more related to job content, which Herzberg labeled "motivating factors."

Herzberg's hygiene-motivation theory has since been debated, tested, criticized, and retested widely. William Winpisinger, the outspoken leader of the International Association of Machinists and Aerospace Workers, gave the union view. "To enrich the job, just enrich the paycheck. The better the wage, the greater the job satisfaction; there is no better cure for the 'blue collar blues.' "

In recent years, however, the expanding content of labor demands, which include more and more perquisites, would seem to validate at least some of Herzberg's findings.

The Productivity Issue

One of the questions left unresolved by Herzberg's researchers concerned productivity and how to predict it in terms of the hygiene-motivation theory. Unfortunately, nearly thirty years have passed without a reliable or credible answer. Some feel that there is little relationship between worker satisfaction and productivity.

At this point, the leader who has to evaluate each follower and decide how work assignments should be distributed for the most productive results is entitled to feel confused.

In our own travels down this same bumpy road, we believe we have developed an approach that can remove much of the guesswork and all of the paranoia. Our *productivity grid* is illustrated in Figure 13.

Rather than puzzling endlessly over whether *hygienes* or *motivators* are the more potent influences over a particular follower in a particular situation, we reasoned that placing these two factors as axes at right angles to form a grid might well simplify the task of allocating responsibilities and assigning tasks.

In other words, we reasoned, that Herzberg's "two different kinds of need/desires" are found in different proportions in nearly everyone. So, rather than setting up an either/or situation to determine which has the greater influence upon productivity, it makes sense to us to blend them by means of a grid. The resulting quadrants can guide us in advantageously using follower tendencies to make decisions about the proper deployment of human resources.

Figure 13.   The productivity grid.

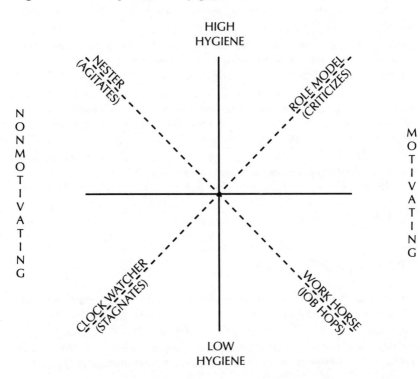

Following are the two kinds of factors identified by the Herzberg research, in approximate order of popular choice:

Hygienes

1. Considerate supervision
2. Good pension
3. High pay
4. Clear company policy
5. Clean working conditions
6. Job security
7. High position
8. Pleasant relationships
9. Job with security

Motivators

1. Job with important purpose
2. Achievement opportunities
3. High pay
4. Recognition for good work
5. Advancement and promotion
6. Job allows participation and decision making
7. Job responsibility
8. Job that stretches you
9. Freedom to organize own time

Note that Herzberg has "high pay" on both lists and, as one might expect, very near the top of each.

Interpreting the Grid

At the top of the grid's vertical axis in Figure 13 is *high hygiene;* at the bottom, *low hygiene.* Similarly, at the left end of the grid's horizontal axis, we find *nonmotivating,* at the right end, *motivating.*

The resulting four quadrants are far more applicable to individuals in a productive environment than the two nine-point lists of factors. This will be apparent as we consider each quadrant separately.

Individuals in the lower-left quadrant are comparatively easy to identify:

- They are usually few in number, thus are conspicuous.

- They are relatively uninterested in either hygiene or motivating factors and don't respond much to either one.
- Productivity holds little interest for them.
- Some are preoccupied by retirement plans.
- A fitting label for this group is *clock-watchers*.
- When dissatisfied, they tend to *stagnate*.

The next easiest individual to identify is in the upper-right quadrant:

- Regrettably, they are rarely present in large numbers;
- They respond openly and positively to both hygiene and motivating factors—they want it all.
- They can keep their eyes on many balls simultaneously.
- Many of the most productive followers are in this quadrant.
- A fitting label for this group is *role models*.
- When dissatisfied, they are quite capable of being constructively *critical;* therefore, they should be heard.

Individuals in the upper-left quadrant are less easy to identify:

- They are inclined to keep a low profile, a trait some have acquired over their many years in the organization.
- They are usually preoccupied with security.
- If they respond to a leader's efforts at all, it will usually be because of hygiene factors.
- Some have been known to lead rebellions.
- A fitting label for this group is *nesters*.
- When dissatisfied, they are sometimes inclined to *agitate*.

Individuals in the lower-right quadrant are not terribly difficult to spot:

- They are generally the next-most productive group.
- They have comparatively little interest in security.
- They generally respond only to motivating factors.
- A fitting label for this group is *workhorses*.
- When dissatisfied, they might be inclined to *job hop*.

The object of our productivity grid is threefold: to identify tendencies, to anticipate behavior, and to enhance productivity.

Tolerance, Resiliency, Alacrity

One of our concerns in advocating the use of the productivity grid is that it not become a counterproductive tool. A leader who is intolerant of others or who does not possess a capacity for resiliency when things don't go as planned can create unnecessary problems. In using the grid, such leaders might be inclined simply to ignore all those in quadrants other than the one in which they place themselves.

This is wrong. An inescapable leadership obligation is to get the very best contributions from all involved without regard for their quadrant. Indeed, it is quite possible to offer opportunities for a significant number to learn to operate in the upper-right quadrant along the way. Getting a follower's best effort and simultaneously inspiring a move to a more productive quadrant calls for the highest order of motivation by the leader. For such purpose, we recommend a review of our concept of the skill of motivation and where we feel motivation begins—the "G" word—and ends—the "P" word.

Enlightened leaders know that each quadrant is likely to be well represented within the ranks of their followers and that various individuals are quite capable of moving gradually from one quadrant to another. Such movement should be both expected and used to advantage, which brings us to a favorite Churchill quotation: "If you're young and not liberal, you have no heart; but, if you're old and not conservative—no brain!"

There are no absolute cinches in the business of leadership, enlightened or otherwise. You may carefully put labels on each follower, but they may all fall off. It takes enormous tenacity and resiliency to reorient your thinking under such conditions and to act with the same alacrity as when all goes according to plan.

APPLICATION METHOD 6

Generating Autotelism Through Ignition, Assimilation, and Empowerment

The Autotelic Experience

Those who are self-fulfilled by what they do are said to have found autotelism. The college professor who instructs students in order to make them more successful in later life is not autotelic, but one who teaches merely to enjoy the experience as an end in itself meets the autotelic definition.

From the former chairman of the Department of Psychology at the University of Chicago, Dr. Mihaly Csikszentmihalyi, we learn that:

> The term autotelic derives from two Greek words, *auto* meaning self and *telos* meaning goal. It refers to a self-contained activity, one that is done not with the expectation of some future benefit, but simply that the doing itself is the reward. . . . Most things we do are neither purely autotelic nor purely exotelic (as we shall call activities done for external reasons only), but are a combination of the two.

The leaders with autotelic followers are the most likely to turn out notable achievement. The ability to generate a sense of self-fullfillment in their followers, therefore, is a worthy aim for all leaders.

Such a state of self-satisfaction may be impossible for some people ever to achieve, and there is no certain way of knowing in advance which followers will and which will not respond. It becomes a matter of perseverance and patience on the part of the leader to make it happen for as many as possible. And all the while, the enlightened leader will be eagerly on the lookout for those candidates for autotelic behavior who also meet the description of the eupsychian participant described by Dr. Abraham H. Maslow in his book *Eupsychian Management*. Maslow described *eupsychian* as a representative of a "culture that would be generated by 1,000 self-actualized people on some sheltered island where they would not be interfered with . . . a play on the word 'utopian' . . . or, in an ideal psychological environment."

A three-phase approach is recommended to leaders who aspire to develop autotelic followers, as illustrated here:

Phase 3: Empowerment
Phase 2: Assimilation
Phase 1: Ignition

Phase 1: Ignition

The first step on the way to ignition is to make a follower aware of the superior productivity possible when autotelism is present in the dynamics of a leader/follower effort. It is a formidable assignment for the leader to see that each follower learns what it feels like not to experience fatigue at the end of a long day on the job. There is no way to prescribe which motivational tactics should be employed in every case. Further, each person's motivation can vary from time to time.

An enlightened leader, having experienced the phenomenon already through the very act of leadership, will know that transferring such a precious quality rarely happens instantly in large numbers, as it does in the tabernacle of a charismatic evangelist. But it can and often does occur on a one-to-one basis, perhaps initially with a follower who has the capacity to become the leader someday.

Once this "super-follower" has been imbued with the concept, the leader will have a partner to help in igniting others. (Remember: "Tell me, I'll forget; show me, I may remember; involve me, I'll involve others!") Thus it may well be necessary to pick them off and ignite them one at a time, since *autotelism* will be nothing more than a strange new word to the group. And, of course, it will take energy and enthusiasm. A laid-back leader is an oxymoron.

Nancy Austin, coauthor with Tom Peters of *A Passion for Excellence*, goes around the country advocating the death of bureaucracy in business organizations. She says they're going to have to become more horizontal, that is, with fewer vertical layers.

Peters himself, in *Thriving On Chaos*, is even more vociferous. If U.S. business is to remain competitive in world markets, he believes, leaders must communicate at the "front line" in pursuit of "fast action":

> Let no day pass without acting as a visible model by engaging in at least one feat of bureaucracy destruction . . . Rant and rave. Tear up papers. Refuse to read them. Don't attend meetings. Just get it done. . . . Regardless of how deeply you buy and live this message, you will still act like a bureaucrat and turf guardian several times a day. That's wonderful news, because it means you can unfailingly preface an attack on others with an attack on yourself. At each weekly staff meeting, consider including a "report card" on yourself. Cite your violations: paperwork excess, turf guardianship, and so on . . . Give people hell, lightheartedly (present a duncecap) or in earnest . . . Have a different person present a report card on you as a whole each week.

One of the risks in anointing one or more of the group is the danger of being caught playing favorites. More than twenty years ago, a little book came out about gaining power with people through better people knowledge. *Power With People* was a layman's answer to the rash of self-help volumes being published at the time that, almost as one voice, were preaching abstractions of psychological theory for achieving success. Toward the end of this book, its author, James K. Van Fleet, offers this advice:

> Never play favorites—when you start to make exceptions to the rule because of some personal preference, the rest of the people will immediately adopt a "don't give a damn" attitude toward you and what you want.
>
> If you pass over a man who should've been promoted in favor of someone who's obviously not as well qualified, you're destroying your power with people. I know of nothing else that will so rapidly undermine your position as your unfairness or your partiality toward some individual or group.

Play favorites, and the unfavored hate you as much as they hate the favored one. That's how Joseph ended up in Egypt. He was his father's favorite son and he rubbed his brothers' noses in the dirt just once too often with his coat of many colors, his dreams, and his visions of power over them.

So they "sold Joseph to the Ishmeelites for twenty pieces of silver: and they brought Joseph into Egypt." Don't allow your emotions or your private prejudices to creep into your decisions about people. You should carefully avoid any prejudices of race, creed, or color if you want to treat every one fairly and gain power with people.

So where does all this leave you as you pursue the vital leadership function of igniting your followers to catch the spark of autotelism? On the one hand, you need apprentice leaders; on the other hand, you dare not risk playing favorites. Fortunately, there is a way out of this dilemma. It's a simple concept, but for some reason it eludes many otherwise competent executives all of their lives: The fact is that *if you will be just a little observant, the group will finger their own cocaptains for you.*

Sometimes, the selection is not even subtle, but at other times, it's necessary to validate the group's silent nominees with tests of your own. But it happens—that's for sure. Take it and run, because, together with the group's self-selected leaders you can and you will in time be victorious in your quest for *ignition*.

Phase 2: Assimilation

Before productive behavior in any realm can become a reality, there has to be a genuine and full assimilation of the necessary and basic ingredients of the task at hand by the members of the group. This is not to suggest that each follower must study each and every bend in the road before setting out on a journey. What we are saying, nonetheless, is that, taking a NASA flight crew as an example, the leader will not have succeeded in empowering the crew to perform until there is clear evidence that they have indeed assimilated the key routines involved in achieving a safe voyage. Such detail is almost always absorbed with deliberate care and in very small bites. Implanting such knowledge securely can be a frustrating exercise in itself. Testing and retesting are the leader's watchwords for strongest assimilation.

As a leader, you can have no greater ally in this process than yourself: You must be your own best example. Ask nothing more of a follower than what you yourself are quite willing and able to do: "Example is leadership," said Albert Schweitzer.

When it comes to facilitating the followers' *assimilation* of knowledge, little more need be said except that the process can prove to be unending and quite cluttered. According to Tom Peters:

> The world today is uniquely "messy," with a host of new variables surfacing at lightning speed. The manager had better be as "messy" as the world; that is, she or he must have an undistorted feel for the uncertainties out there on the line. Information-processing scientists even have a term to describe this need: "requisite variety." That is, the variety of your sources must match the complexity of the real problem, or you will be led to erroneous conclusions."

Awareness of the peril of clutter in the followers' *assimilation* process will make for a stronger leader/follower bonding.

Phase 3: Empowerment

Empowerment is the granting of power and/or authority. We're getting serious now! But *empowerment* must happen in the implementation of truly enlightened leadership. The alternatives are not pleasant. One is complete consternation for the unenlightened leader who tries, like the honeybee, to pollinate all the flowers alone, rather than bestowing such duties upon others whose idleness will only activate their stingers.

In any event, enlightened followership is what the enlightened leader will be looking for in coming to grips with the bottom-line question: How and when can one empower others to share in the power and authority of the leader on behalf of predetermined common objectives?

An affirmative response to these queries need not signal an endless contest for greater status or larger and larger vestiges of delegated authority. It will mean that power has become what Warren Bennis and Burt Nanus call a "unit of exchange—an active, changing token in creative, productive, and communicative transactions. Effective leaders will ultimately reap the human harvest of their efforts by the simple action of power's reciprocal: empowerment."

Reciprocal empowerment generates its own kind of rhythm, its own vitality and momentum. It often results in the forming of even stronger allegiances and compound recommitments that might never have otherwise occurred. Of course, there can also be the rare instance when an immature follower, perhaps intoxicated with newly acquired power, attempts to run up the chest and down the back of a leader who has been wrongly perceived to be overly permissive. But such a slight risk should not deter you from the vital act of empowering others who have given evidence of their readiness for such trust.

What really goes on in the complete *empowerment* process is a building of dependency in the beginning, followed by a relinquishing of control and an enabling of greater independence as time goes on.

The results of enlightened leadership can be seen in the attitudes of the led. Bennis and Nanus suggest that such attitudes may reflect one or more of these four critical dimensions:

1. The feeling of being at the active center
2. The feeling that one's competence is being enhanced
3. The feeling of belonging to something akin to "family," joined in some common purpose
4. A feeling of just plain enjoyment—FUN!

With this kind of *empowerment* in place, enlightened leaders will be much better prepared to apply successfully the six skills or, for that matter, any others.

So there you have it—our Six Methods for more effective Application of Leadership Skills:

Method 6: Ignition—Assimilation—Empowerment!
Method 5: Applying the "Productivity Grid."
Method 4: Four key personal considerations.
Method 3: The four dynamics of leadership.
Method 2: Willingness, the first action component.
Method 1: Nearly all have the potential.

PART SIX

Leadership Priorities

(How the Enlightened Leader Chooses)

There are always more convincing arguments to do nothing than compelling reasons to take action.

—Anonymous

Endowed with a balanced awareness of our six proven leadership *principles*, six leadership *skills*, and six techniques for *applying* them, the candidate for leadership will doubtless find numerous mountains to climb and possibly even a world or two to conquer. This prospect recalls those blockbuster questions from the Preface, all of which relate to the central leadership quandary: How do you evaluate *leadership priorities*? Because no one can—nor should one even try to—put out all fires.

By way of review, the inevitable questions that must be answered again and again by everyone who aspires to lead are:

- Who am I really?
- Why am I here?
- In what am I rooted?
- How large is my potential?
- How do I make it happen?

Once again, before addressing these questions, we must offer some caveats:

First, many of those who elect to adopt our format of principles/ skills/application techniques may well have little if any trouble in evaluating which *leadership priorities* to pursue.

Second, some who elect to adopt our format simply may never actually be confronted with more than one leadership challenge at a time.

Third, some who elect to adopt our format may find that our method of evaluating priorities is not, perhaps for personal reasons, the desired course of action to follow.

Fourth, there may be some who reject our format altogether and thus need read no further.

It is the third group above that gives us greatest concern. Within this category, who can be sure how many simply feel that, regardless of the soundness of our approaches to leadership, if they were meant to lead, fate would have opened the way long ago. We remind those who might be so inclined of the strong ecumenical support for "anti-fatalism" down through the years. After all, we do have choices; we are always making them.

Many who aspire to be leaders must inevitably determine which of numerous alternative leadership opportunities to pursue. The more fortunate ones will have little difficulty. Perhaps they will advance along a career path already before them or will make a long-anticipated career change that seemed too threatening before. Perhaps those already in leadership roles will be able to step out with greater confidence.

Ultimately, however, many who have the capacity to lead will be confronted with several competing causes from which to choose, often with very little time to evaluate the many considerations involved. In such circumstances, some will be tempted and/or pressed to take on several leadership challenges at the same time. When this happens, the result can be very real frustration, either from letting go of one or more of the opportunities to lead or from taking on more than can possibly be done successfully by one person. Dillon Anderson, an old friend of ours, once said he had found the perfect solution to such a dilemma: "Just don't take yourself so seriously!" But, he mused, "That, for me, never lasted very long. I soon found that I finally had to be tough enough with myself to ask, 'Who do you think you are?' I had to realize quite often that I couldn't put out all fires and that I would have to be content with merely starting a few."

Isn't it fascinating that the managing partner of one of the nation's leading law firms, board chairman of a large regional bank, secretary of the National Security Council in the Eisenhower administration, and a director of major corporations like Monsanto and Union

Oil—who also found time to become a popular author—would have to inquire who he thought he was rather than to bludgeon himself with still one more leadership commitment? And this is a man who instinctively lived and breathed our leadership principles, who had mastered leadership skills, and who modeled much of our technique for skills application. One key to his success is that no challenge could plague him for long, once he had tested it in the crucible of his deep convictions and had made an evaluation of whatever it might involve in terms of his available personal resources. And then with complete confidence he made a decision!

Who Am I?

How do most of the rest of us go about making these decisions? Do we really test our options against our deep convictions? Indeed, do we have any genuinely deep convictions?

What happens all too often is that we habitually turn to what they—whoever they may be—would have us think . . . do . . . and eventually become. Much of our lives seems to be a matter of seeking an identity, which after all is a matter of identifying one's core convictions. What is left when temporal things change? In Leadership Myth 11, we cited the words of S. I. Hayakawa concerning the peril of becoming a victim of one's own culture as one's independence wanes. And so it is again here, we think, a matter of focus upon individuality and deeper convictions.

Our thrust in Part Six is certainly not that each reader must become a world-beater with the deep convictions of a saint. But we do hold that learning who you really are in terms of your core beliefs can be the straightest possible track on which to guide your activities, especially those involving leadership.

We have now virtually come back full circle to Leadership Principle 1: Self-Knowledge. The following approach illustrates how uncomplicated and thoroughly revealing the process can be.

Let's say you have just made a new acquaintance . . . someone you almost immediately feel you would like to have as a personal friend . . . and she asks without warning, "Who are you, anyway?"

Most of us would flounder a bit in trying to answer such a simple but wide-ranging question, and our reply would be somewhat disorganized. For the purposes of this book, where you have no one looking over your shoulder as you read, we suggest you take paper and pencil in hand and begin writing a list of the ten key things that form a picture of who you are. Please do this now. . . .

With list in hand, with some deletions and perhaps some under-
scores of important points, please answer the following questions:

1. Did you tell what you do . . . have done . . . will do?
2. Do the most important items come first, last, or in no particular order?
3. How many items involve personal relationships (married, single, parents, children, etc.) versus public relationships (group
   involvement, projects, causes, etc.)
4. Which of the following are featured . . . or perhaps omitted
   entirely:
   • Religious preference?
   • Political preference?
   • Professional preference?
   • Cultural activities?
   • Physiological needs?
   • Intellectual interests?
   • Psychological needs?
5. Are there contradictions on your list?
6. Which items are really essential? Which are relatively inci-
   dental?
7. Would *you* want *you* for a friend?

Don't be surprised at two basic conclusions. First, if you're like
most people, you have only a limited understanding of yourself, usually confined to a few isolated phases of your life. Second, the assessment points up the dichotomy between the way you actually live and
the way you would like to live.

If your list and our seven questions leave you somewhat frustrated, please try making another list—but only after you've finished
Part Six. Then ask yourself the same seven questions.

Why Am I Here?

Within each of us are the necessary sparks to do just about whatever
we're bold enough to try. Who is to say precisely what ignites human
achievement? Was Thomas Edison predestined? . . . Albert Einstein?
. . . or Susan B. Anthony? Were other greats and near-greats locked
onto career paths over which they held little personal control? Or did
each of these models of productive humankind make conscious—
even laborious—efforts to do what they did?

Whether they did or not in each case is hardly the issue. The point is that the answer to why we are actually here lies very much in our own hands. How to go about determining the answer depends upon the complexity of the circumstances surrounding the objective in prospect. One thing is absolutely certain: Few achievements of magnitude in any field have been reached or even approached without painstaking preparation. And as you prepare for whatever task you want to undertake—be it large or small—we urge you not to become a victim of fatalism, accepting that *whatever will be will be.*

In C. P. Snow's novel *The Light and the Dark,* a tormented character is convinced that everything has been decided long in advance and that all preparation and effort are useless. What a tragic world in which to live, for some to be destined for life in the fullest while others, no matter how desperately they try, are to be denied most of life's rewards.

Even the sixteenth-century Protestant reformer John Calvin would have branded such a belief "double predestination"—that is, "some are included, some are excluded." We affirm the significance of human decision making concerning our mortal choices and actions, but this is not intended to deny the sovereignty of the Deity. Rather, we humans are completely free to discover why we are actually here through the exercise of a purposeful will, all in harmony with our own individual convictions, spiritual and otherwise.

What more enabling outlook could anyone possibly have? Yet, why is acting upon this outlook so difficult? Might it be because those convictions we keep coming back to are so torn and muddled within us? If so, the next section will surely be useful.

In What Am I Truly Rooted?

In our earlier discussion of self-knowledge, we noted that a major job placement firm in San Diego customarily surveys the personal values of all applicants. The idea is to form an impression of each individual's innermost beliefs—his or her *value system*—as a guide to what fields and job descriptions might best deserve consideration.

Similarly, as you go about the task of choosing how and where to make your commitments to leadership, it is incumbent upon you to attempt to identify those values and convictions in which you are truly rooted.

"Where do I begin?" you may ask. Following are ten indicators for appraising your personality, each in the form of a question. This guide to self-analysis was developed by Dr. Murray Banks, world famous lecturer who has brought his message on "How To Live With

Yourself" to more than 5,000 audiences in every English-speaking country in the world:

1. *Are you happy?* Happiness comes as a by-product of effectively striving for desirable goals. . . . Don't confuse it with pleasure . . . pleasure you can buy . . . but happiness can't be bought . . . it must be lived . . . it comes as a reward for good living.
2. *Are you ambitious for life?* Do you have a zest for living? . . . Some people of 80 and 90 years are very young . . . others at 18 and 19 are very old . . . some merely eke out their existence. . . . Life is something we create. . . . Be ambitious . . . but don't frustrate yourself with impossible goals.
3. *Are you socially adjusted?* Do you like people? Do you get along well with others? One who hates people and enjoys a completely solitary life does not enjoy mental health.
4. *Do you have unity and balance?* You are not always torn between choices . . . you are moderate in all things . . . you do not wrap your entire life around any one thing . . . even a mother, father, wife, husband, or child. . . . Don't lose your balance by attempting to please everyone . . . unless, of course, you want to end up as a good neurotic. . . . Criticism is usually a sign that you are alive and doing things.
5. *Do you give attention in your life to the present?* We make a hell on earth worrying about the past . . . by regretting and regressing . . . by wishing we could do it over . . . or undo it all. . . . An elderly man once said: "I am an old man and have had many troubles, most of which never happened. . . ." Worry, worry, worry . . . worry over the past . . . worry over the future . . . little consideration for the present.
6. *Do you have insight into your own conduct?* Insight is the quality of being able to see into yourself . . . and see the truth . . . and understand the deeper reasons for your behavior. . . . A psychiatrist doesn't attempt to cure you . . . but to help you to help yourself. . . . The only thing in this world that can hurt you is not what you know, but what you don't know. . . . Ignorance isn't bliss!
7. *Do you have a confidential relationship with someone?* Every person—no matter how old, young, rich, poor, or successful— needs someone in whom to confide. . . . Loneliness is a cancer. . . . A sorrow shared is always halved . . . a joy shared is always doubled. . . . Some need a listener so badly, they even get married . . . then often comes the greatest irony of

all, that the very person they sought to talk to freely and honestly becomes the one they deceive.

8. *Do you have a sense of the ridiculous?* This is more than just a sense of humor . . . can you laugh at yourself? Beware of feeling too important . . . there is always someone who feels more important than you do. . . . A patient in a mental ward struck an exaggerated pose . . . a psychiatrist passing by said, "Who do you think you are?" . . . "Napoleon," came the reply. "Who told you that?" "The Lord told me." "I certainly did not!"came a voice from the next bed.

9. *Are you engaged in satisfying work?* Not everyone is, you know. . . . Satisfying work can be a most positive influence for mental hygiene . . . it's a strong prop for weathering life's many frustrations. . . . Fortunate, indeed, are those who discover early what their niche in life should be . . . and who eventually become actively engaged in work they would gladly do for nothing.

10. *Do you attack your problems promptly and intelligently?* We are not in trouble . . . trouble is in us. . . . Do something active about the cause of your worry . . . and when you can't, seek a "balancing factor." . . . Bing Crosby's son was feeling very sad because his pet turtle was dying, and Bing had tried to cheer him up: "Look, son, if the turtle dies, here's what we will do: we'll put him in a nice box, get all the kids together, put on fancy uniforms, get a bugle, march down the street in a parade and bury him in the backyard!" . . . Nathaniel listened silently and finally said: "Let's kill him!"

Do these ten indicators bring you a little closer to identifying some of your core beliefs? Whatever your response, we submit still another approach for probing further into your value system and the convictions in which it is rooted. This approach comes from the book *Bi-Polar, A Positive Way of Understanding People*, written by J. W. Thomas, popular southwestern management consultant. His basic thesis is that "all creativity is a blend of opposites; what makes for real strength in a person is the blending of two opposite strengths." Thomas sets up a number of categories, including:

- Reason/emotion
- Analysis/intuition
- Reality/imagination
- Head/heart

- Left brain/right brain
- Thinking/feeling

A judicious blend of these bi/polar qualities offers a revealing approach toward a better understanding of oneself.

And that, after all, is what we're seeking, a better understanding of self! So, if blending one's thoughts and feelings is the key to better self-understanding and creativity, let's use this as a criterion to analyze our value systems and learn that in which we are truly rooted.

In order to stimulate the process, we offer the following collection of our favorite quotations on *thinking* and *feeling*. Any one (or combination) of the following sentiments is capable of triggering one's old convictions and thus perhaps leading to the development of new ones.

Six Super-Sentiments on Thinking

1. "Be grateful for ideas that use you."—Cicero
2. "In the end, thought rules the world. There are times when impulses and passions seem more powerful, but they soon expend themselves; while mind, acting constantly, is ever ready to drive them back and work reliably when emotional energy is exhausted."—J. McCash
3. "We think too small. Like the frog at the bottom of the well. He thinks the sky is only as big as the top of the well. If he surfaced, he would have an entirely different view."—Mao Tse-tung
4. "Few people think more than two or three times a year. I have made an international reputation for myself by thinking once or twice a week."—George Bernard Shaw
5. "It is much easier to think right without doing right, than to do right without thinking right."—Hare
6. "Thought engenders thought. Place one idea upon paper, another will follow it—and often still another—until you have written a page. You cannot fathom your mind; it is a well of thought which has no bottom. The more you draw from it, the more clear and fruitful it will be. At first, ideas may come out in lumps, homely and shapeless; but no matter. Time and perseverance will arrange and polish them."—G. A. Sala

Six Super-Sentiments on Feeling

1. "A life is feeling and action; it is required of a man that he share the feelings and passions of his time at the peril of being judged not to have lived at all."—Oliver Wendell Holmes

2. "I have friends in overalls whose feelings and friendship I would not swap for the favor of kings."—Thomas A. Edison
3. "Affirmation of life is the spiritual feeling by which men cease to live unreflectively."—Albert Schweitzer
4. "The two most deadly and poisonous feelings of man are avarice and greed."—*The Count of Monte Cristo* (Paramount Pictures, 1934)
5. "If you feel you are indispensable, put your finger in a glass of water, withdraw it, and note the hole you have left."—Anonymous
6. "Only when one has lost all feeling about the future has one reached the age to write an autobiography."—Evelyn Waugh

Finally, here's one that could have made either list:

"Half of our mistakes in life arise from feeling when we ought to think—or thinking when we ought to feel."—John Churton Collins

We shall close this subject with the model core beliefs of W. C. Coleman, inventor of the famous lantern. He had these ten personal qualities printed on small cards that he distributed by the thousands during the closing years of his life.

Personal Qualities That Ensure Success

1. A practical imagination. Every element contributing to human progress is first conceived and visualized in the mind.
2. A pioneering spirit which always believes there are new methods and better things to be discovered.
3. Initiative which impels one to do something about it.
4. Courage to launch out and attempt the seemingly impossible.
5. Resourcefulness that overcomes every difficulty along the way.
6. Persistence, that is, the stamina to carry through to completion.
7. The joy of achievement, which makes hard work a pleasure.
8. Capacity to work with other people; every great achievement requires cooperative effort, and loyalty to a common purpose.
9. A becoming humility which acknowledges the help of others.

10. Qualities of the heart which cause one to find real joy and satisfaction in promoting the welfare of others.

How Large Is My Potential?

Some astronomers theorize that billions of years ago the universe originated in a big bang, the explosion of a single mass, and that since that time, the pieces have been flying apart as the universe expands. On such a scale as this, what microscopic grains of sand our physical beings are! Yet, within each of us is the boundless potential of mind and spirit. In fact, each of us is endowed with a brain capacity of 280 quintillion bytes of information (that's 280,000,000,000,000,000,000,000!)

There are some people who are able to excel individually, as in one of the arts, but most of us become involved with teams of others as we endeavor to produce and achieve. Since random group activity seldom succeeds, leaders must emerge. It is in this context that we seek an answer to the fourth blockbuster question: *How large is my potential?*

That great footlight philosopher Woody Allen got close to the answer when he quipped, "I love those times when I'm about to be creative, but deliver me from when I'm like two with the universe—no one needs to be that much out of step."

The question is, out of step with what? Many believe that the 1990s will be a period of crisis for the United States as Americans try to solve the problems that germinated in the 1970s and '80s. Once a proud and prosperous world power, the United States has become the world's largest debtor nation. Other problems include one of the lowest domestic rates of saving, an estimated $500-billion liability for the S&L mess, a trade imbalance that makes the nation a net exporter of jobs, not goods, a neglected infrastructure, and pressure on our federal, state, and local governments to take up the slack in hiring instead of supporting and strengthening private enterprise (approximately one-third of the U.S. labor force works for federal, state, or local governments). With growing crime, violence, divorce, drug and child abuse, and increasingly expensive medical care, this is hardly the "American Dream." Who would opt to be "in step" with all of this?

Few Americans feel ready to tackle such massive problems personally. But how long can any of us remain indifferent? Laid back leadership is an oxymoron. Three major areas of civic need are *public safety, health care,* and *education.*

In *public safety,* the major problem of course is drugs. As much as

75 percent of urban crime is alcohol- or drug-related. More rehabilitation opportunity must come for lower- and middle-income levels. Business needs to be more assertive in ensuring a drug-free workplace. Neighborhood law enforcement needs the kind of block-by-block leadership that brings police and residents together. Homeless street people also must be rehabilitated.

In *health care*, the overriding issue is cost. There is much more to be done on the administrative side of health care to contain the upward spiral of medical expenses. Few hospitals have all the concerned citizens they can use actively at their board level.

In *education*, what's missing most is something more than mere lip-service to begin to meet our competition abroad. Then there are the chronic problems of poor parental supervision, a growing drop-out rate, and the nation's high levels of illiteracy. Many high school graduates don't know much. One recent survey asked respondents how many sixteenths there are in an inch. Answers included "twelve," "eighteen," and "there are no sixteenths in an inch."

How Do I Make It Happen?

With this final blockbuster question, we perhaps close with a redundancy, having treated self-motivation earlier. But there is a good reason for this: In order to persuade you to fulfill your rendezvous with leadership, we must use every ounce of inducement we can muster.

So, consistent with the modern American's prayer, "Dear God, I pray for patience. And I want it right now," our remaining words shall be guided directly to that end—making your leadership happen. The first step is to review the ground we have covered in this book:

- We have exploded a dozen convenient mythical excuses people use to let leadership go by default.
- We have reviewed what both ancient philosophers and modern researchers have written about leadership.
- We have explored our six proven leadership principles.
- We have examined our six basic leadership skills.
- We have identified six key techniques for applying leadership skills.
- We have begun to examine how effective leaders evaluate their opportunities for leading in terms of their own individual value systems.

We have now reached the point of presenting ways to use all of the information in this book about leadership. To keep things basic, we will summarize our thoughts on how to make leadership happen under two fundamental categories: *attitude* and *action*.

Concerning Attitude

To change your attitude means to change your life. Do you know anyone who is truly comfortable with change? Indeed, in the words of motivational philosopher Ray Z-M Blitzer, "The only person who likes change is a wet baby!" Along with change comes a companion word—that dreaded four-letter word, *risk*. The problem is that change plus risk produces fear. Here are three pertinent paragraphs from Dr. Susan Jeffers' book *Feel the Fear and Do It Anyway:*

> One of the biggest fears that keeps us from moving ahead with our lives is our difficulty in making decisions. As one of my students lamented, "Sometimes I feel like the proverbial donkey between two bales of hay—unable to decide which one I want, and, in the meantime, starving to death." The irony, of course, is that by not choosing, we are choosing—to starve. We are choosing to deprive ourselves of what makes life a delicious feast.
>
> The problem is that we have been taught "Be careful! You might make the wrong decision!" A wrong decision! Just the sound of that can bring terror to our hearts. We are afraid that the wrong decision will deprive us of something—money, friends, lovers, status, or whatever the right decision is supposed to bring us.
>
> Closely tied to this is our panic over making mistakes. For some reason we feel we should be perfect, and forget that we learn through our mistakes. Our need to be perfect and our need to control the outcome of events work together to keep us petrified when we think about making a change or attempting a new challenge.

All of this fear and all of this worry is needless, according to Dr. Jeffers. She writes, "All you have to do to change your world is change the way you think about it. . . . The knowledge that you can handle anything that comes your way is the key to allowing yourself to take risks."

Her reference to risks in this context, we are quite sure, means reasonable risks that carry the promise of meaningful reward. No one would advocate the reckless acceptance of foolhardy risks. In the end, each individual has the option of using his or her own initiative to attain the winning *attitude* necessary to make leadership happen. And when it does happen, the effective leader is able to then consider *actions* that can add wholeness to living.

On one of his Careertrack Publications' audio cassettes, Lou Heckler sums it all up with a question: "Do you realize that the tiny, microscopic, infinitesimal sperm that sparked your life in your mother's womb had to outswim more than eight million others? Brother," he goes on, "with ancestry like that, *you gotta be a winner!*"

Somehow, we think that may be just about all anyone needs to know about *attitude*.

Concerning Action

Can you remember the time when you were center stage in the final two minutes of the third act of your senior class play and you forgot your lines? Your mind went blank . . . the audience shifted in their seats . . . your entire life passed before your eyes . . . your mother passed out.

But then, from offstage, there came a cue word. And that's the *action* we would have you take right now. Please write down our cue word for making leadership happen in your life. That word, with only four letters, is *rope* . . . R–O–P–E. We care not where you write it. But if you're really serious, write it on half a dozen 3- by 5-inch cards to put in key spots (like your top bureau drawer), where you'll see them for routine reminders at various times during a typical day.

Why *rope?* For the answer, see Figure 14, which is a letter from a Phoenix bricklayer to the Arizona State Compensation Fund.

If you are willing to risk the acceptance of the leadership mantle on the terms we have suggested, you will realize its rich promises and its deep inner rewards. But, unlike the bricklayer, you must hold onto your ropes:

- The rope you now hold as one who understands our six basic leadership principles
- The rope that six proven leadership skills place firmly in your hands

Figure 14.   A classic lesson in perseverance.

State Compensation Fund   October 3, 1988
1616 W. Adams Street
Phoenix, Arizona 85005

Dear Sir:

I am writing in response to your request for additional information. In Block 3 of the accident report form, I put "poor planning" as the cause of my accident. You said in your letter that I should explain more fully, and I trust that the following details will be sufficient.

I am a bricklayer by trade. On the day of the accident, I was working alone on the roof of a new six story building. When I completed my work, I discovered that I had about 500 pounds of brick left over.

Rather than carry the bricks down by hand, I decided to lower them in a barrel by using a pulley which unfortunately was attached on the side of the building at the sixth floor.

Securing the rope at ground level, I went up to the roof, swung the barrel out and loaded the brick into it. Then I went back to the ground and untied the rope holding it tightly to insure a slow descent of the 500 pounds of brick. You will note in block number eleven of the accident reporting form that I weigh 135 pounds.

Due to my surprise of being jerked off the ground so suddenly, <u>I lost my presence of mind and forgot to let go of the rope</u>. Needless to say, I proceeded at a rather rapid rate up the side of the building.

In the vicinity of the third floor, I met the barrel coming down. This explains the fractured skull and broken collarbone.

Slowed only slightly, I continued my rapid ascent, not stopping until the fingers of my right hand were two knuckles deep into the pulley. Fortunately, by this time I had regained my presence of mind and was able to hold tightly to the rope in spite of my pain.

At approximately the same time, however, the barrel of bricks hit the ground and the bottom fell out of the barrel. Devoid of the weight of the bricks, the barrel now weighed approximately fifty pounds.

I refer you again to my weight in block number eleven. As you might imagine, I began a rapid descent down the side of the building. In the vicinity of the third floor, I met the barrel coming up. This accounts for the two fractured ankles and the lacerations on my legs and lower body.

The encounter with the barrel slowed me enough to lessen my injuries when I fell onto the pile of bricks and, fortunately, only three vertebrae were cracked.

I am sorry to report, however, that as I lay there on the bricks—in pain, unable to stand, and watching the empty barrel six stories above me—I again lost my presence of mind . . .

<u>I let go of the rope</u> . . .

- The rope links you to six effective techniques for leadership skills application
- The rope links you inexorably to your finest future as an enlightened leader.

Not incidentally, these ropes require *no magic* on your part at all. We are definitely not dealing here with blarney or snake-oil.

What About Luck?

Notwithstanding the entire thrust of this book, that *no magic* is needed to be a leader, we're reluctant to close without consideration of another outside agency: not *magic*, but *luck*! In the words of Machiavelli, "Fortune is the ruler of half our actions, but she allows the other half or thereabouts to be ruled by us." On a more basic level is the view of an anonymous rodeo cowboy: "Luck is where opportunity meets preparation. Opportunity is drawing a good calf. Preparation is having tied enough calves in fast time at home that you'll repeat when the money's down."

Clearly, the concept of luck can be both an enormous windfall or convenient excuse for failure. Since it can never be eliminated, it should never be ignored. In his classic book *How Managers Make Things Happen,* Dr. George S. Odiorne offers these words of wisdom:

> One of the persuasive arguments for luck as a factor in management success is the lack of uniformity in management practices which brought success to one organization and disaster to another. One firm follows all the textbook rules of management in such things as organizing, planning, controlling, motivating, and developing people. It would be a joy to the case writer from the university School of Business Administration. Yet it staggers along with mediocre growth and profit while another without a bit of attention to these things coins vast profits and grows at an exponential rate.

Dr. Odiorne goes on to account for such differences with examples of "keeping abreast of latest trends" . . . "predicting hot items of the future" . . . "planning for the unexpected." He concludes that "The quality which seems most associated with the lucky executive is not one of forbearance and restraint. It is performance and action."

Our own view is that unless your "performance and action" are preceded by *prudent preparation,* "forbearance and restraint" may well be the better course. For there is indeed a high correlation between preparation and luck, where leadership and your ultimate felicity are concerned.

"Within yourself lies the cause of whatever enters your life. To come into full realization of your own awakened interior powers, is to be able to condition your life in exact accord with what you would have it."—Ralph Waldo Trine

Finally, whenever you see one of those R–O–P–E cards and you're reminded of all four of those crucial ropes you held in your hands, think, too, of this acronym:

R — is a cautious reminder of the *Risks* that inevitably will be associated with any and all of your leadership ventures.

O — is for what we hope will be your many *Opportunities* to lead.

P — is for what we trust will be numerous willing *Participants* along the way.

E — is for the *Energy* your leadership can generate in others . . . and, again, it will require *no magic* on your part at all.

Bibliography

Arnold, John D. *Make Up Your Mind*. New York: AMACOM, 1978.

Banks, Murray. *How to Live With Yourself*. New York: Murmil Associates, Inc., 1959.

Bass, Bernard M. *Bass and Stogdill's Handbook of Leadership, Third Edition*. New York: The Free Press, 1990.

———. "From Transactional to Transformational Leadership." *AMA Quarterly Review* (Winter 1990), p. 22.

Bell, John Fred. *A History of Economic Thought*. New York: Ronald Press, 1967.

Benge, Eugene J. *How to Use Your Physical and Emotional Ability to Overcome Your Problems and Realize Your Goals*. Homewood, Ill.: Business One Irwin, 1977).

Bennis, Warren. *The Unconscious Conspiracy*. New York: AMACOM, 1976.

Bennis, Warren, and Burt Nanus. *Leaders*. New York: Harper & Row, 1985.

Burns, David D. *Feeling Good*. New York: New American Library, 1980.

Churchill, Winston S. *The Second World War: Triumph and Tragedy*. Cambridge, Mass.: The Riverside Press, 1953.

Cronin, Thomas E. "Thinking and Learning About Leadership." *Presidential Studies Quarterly* (1984), pp. 22–34.

Csikszentmihalyi, Mihaly. *Flow*. New York: Harper & Row, 1991.

D'Aprix, Roger M. *How's That Again?* Homewood, Ill.: Business One Irwin, 1971.

Drucker, Peter F. *The Effective Executive*. New York: Harper & Row, 1966.

———. *The Practice of Management*. New York: Harper & Row, 1955.

Fournies, Ferdinand F. *Why Employees Don't Do What They're Supposed to Do and What to Do About It.* Blue Ridge Summit, Penn.: Tab Books, 1988.

Frohman, Mark. "Participative Management." *Industry Week* (May 2, 1988), p. 242.

Gabarro, John J., and John P. Kotter. "Managing Your Boss." *Harvard Business Review* (January–February 1980), pp. 94–100.

Geneen, Harold. *Managing.* Garden City, N.Y.: Doubleday & Co., 1989.

George, Claude S., Jr. *The History of Management Thought.* Englewood Cliffs, N.J.: Prentice Hall, 1968.

Haberler, G. "Joseph Alois Schumpeter." *Quarterly Journal of Economics* (August 1950), p. 333.

Hagberg, Janet, and Richard Leider. *The Inventurers.* Reading, Mass.: Addison-Wesley, 1978.

Hart, Hornell. *Autoconditioning.* Englewood Cliffs, N.J.: Prentice Hall, 1956.

Heckler, Lou. *Leadership Training.* Boulder, Colorado: CareerTrack Publications, 1987.

Helgesen, Sally. *Female Advantage: Women's Ways of Leadership.* New York: Doubleday & Co., 1990.

Hickman, Craig R. *Mind of a Manager, Soul of a Leader.* New York: John Wiley & Sons, 1990.

Hind, James F. *The Heart and Soul of Effective Management.* New York: Victor Books, 1989.

Hyatt, Carole, and Linda Gottlieb. *When Smart People Fail.* New York: Penguin Books, 1988.

Jeffers, Susan. *Feel the Fear and Do It Anyway.* New York: Harcourt Brace Jovanovich, 1987.

Kushner, Harold S. *When All You've Ever Wanted Isn't Enough.* New York: Summit Books, 1986.

Laborde, Genie Z. *Influencing With Integrity.* Palo Alto, Calif.: Syntony Publishing, 1987.

Locke, Edwin A., and Gary P. Latham. *Goal Setting.* New York: AMACOM, 1979.

Lundy, James L. *Lead, Follow, or Get Out of the Way.* San Diego: Avant Books, 1986.

Maslow, Abraham H. *Eupsychian Management.* Homewood, Ill.: Richard D. Irwin, Inc., 1965.

Miller, Sherod, Daniel Wackman, Elam Nunnally, and Phyllis Miller. *Connecting With Self and Others.* Littleton, Colorado: Interpersonal Communication Programs, Inc., 1988.

Odiorne, George S. *How Managers Make Things Happen.* Englewood Cliffs, N.J.: Prentice-Hall, 1961.

Peters, Thomas J. *Thriving On Chaos.* New York: Harper & Row, 1987.

Peters, Thomas J., and Nancy K. Austin. *A Passion for Excellence.* New York: Warner Books, 1985.

Peters, Thomas J., and Robert H. Waterman, Jr. *In Search of Excellence.* New York: Harper & Row, 1982.

Plato. *The Republic.* Translated by Benjamin Jowett. New York: Random House, 1955.

Thomas, J. W. *Bi-Polar, A Positive Way of Understanding People.* Dallas: Taylor Publishing, 1978.

Toffler, Alvin. *Powershift.* New York: Bantam Books, 1990.

Van Fleet, James K. *Power With People.* West Nyack, N.Y.: Parker Publishing, 1970.

———. *The 22 Biggest Mistakes Managers Make and How to Correct Them.* West Nyack, N.Y.: Parker Publishing Company, 1973.

Vroom, Victor H. *Work and Motivation.* New York: John Wiley & Sons, 1964.

Vroom, Victor H., and Arthur G. Jago. *The New Leadership.* Englewood Cliffs, N.J.: Prentice Hall, 1988.

West, Robin L. "How to Build Your Memory Power." *Executive Health Report,* Vol. XXIV, No. 11 (August 1988).

Wilson, Larry. *Personality Grid: Managing Interpersonal Relationships.* Eden Prairie, Minn.: Wilson Learning Corporation, 1978.

———. *Sell-Tell-Jell: Sales Sonics.* Eden Prairie, Minn.: Wilson Learning Corporation, 1969.

Winpisinger, William W. "Job Enrichment: A Union View." *Monthly Labor Review* (April 1973), p. 54.

Wren, Daniel A. *The Evolution of Management Thought.* New York: John Wiley & Sons, 1987.

Zaleznik, Abraham. *The Managerial Mystique.* New York: Harper & Row, 1989.

Index